World Economic and Financial Surveys

WORLD ECONOMIC OUTLOOK
December 2001

The Global Economy After September 11

International Monetary Fund

©2001 International Monetary Fund

Production: IMF Graphics Section
Cover and Design: Luisa Menjivar-Macdonald
Figures: Theodore F. Peters, Jr.
Typesetting: Choon Lee

World economic outlook (International Monetary Fund)
World economic outlook: a survey by the staff of the International
Monetary Fund.—1980– —Washington, D.C.: The Fund, 1980–

v.; 28 cm.—(1981–84: Occasional paper/International Monetary
Fund ISSN 0251-6365)
Annual.
Has occasional updates, 1984–
ISSN 0258-7440 = World economic and financial surveys
ISSN 0256-6877 = World economic outlook (Washington)
1. Economic history—1971– —Periodicals.   I. International
Monetary Fund.   II. Series: Occasional paper (International
Monetary Fund)

HC10.W7979   84-640155

338.5'443'09048—dc19
AACR 2 MARC-S

Library of Congress   8507

Published biannually.
ISBN 1-58906-087-3

Price: US$42.00
(US$35.00 to full-time faculty members and
students at universities and colleges)

Please send orders to:
International Monetary Fund, Publication Services
700 19th Street, N.W., Washington, D.C. 20431, U.S.A.
Tel.: (202) 623-7430   Telefax: (202) 623-7201
E-mail: publications@imf.org
Internet: http://www.imf.org

recycled paper

CONTENTS

Tables

Figures

ASSUMPTIONS AND CONVENTIONS

A number of assumptions have been adopted for the projections presented in the *World Economic Outlook*. It has been assumed that real effective exchange rates will remain constant at their average levels during September 17–October 16, 2001, except for the currencies participating in the European exchange rate mechanism II (ERM II), which are assumed to remain constant in nominal terms relative to the euro; that established policies of national authorities will be maintained; that the average price of oil will be $24.25 a barrel in 2001 and $18.50 a barrel in 2002, and thereafter it is based on market information; and that the six-month London interbank offered rate (LIBOR) on U.S. dollar deposits will average 3.8 percent in 2001 and 2.8 percent in 2002. These are, of course, working hypotheses rather than forecasts, and the uncertainties surrounding them add to the margin of error that would in any event be involved in the projections. The estimates and projections are based on statistical information available through early December, 2001.

The following conventions have been used throughout the *World Economic Outlook*:

. . .   to indicate that data are not available or not applicable;

—   to indicate that the figure is zero or negligible;

–   between years or months (for example, 1997–98 or January–June) to indicate the years or months covered, including the beginning and ending years or months;

/   between years or months (for example, 1997/98) to indicate a fiscal or financial year.

"Billion" means a thousand million; "trillion" means a thousand billion.

"Basis points" refer to hundredths of 1 percentage point (for example, 25 basis points are equivalent to ¼ of 1 percentage point).

In figures and tables, shaded areas indicate IMF staff projections.

Minor discrepancies between sums of constituent figures and totals shown are due to rounding.

As used in this report, the term "country" does not in all cases refer to a territorial entity that is a state as understood by international law and practice. As used here, the term also covers some territorial entities that are not states but for which statistical data are maintained on a separate and independent basis.

FURTHER INFORMATION AND DATA

This report on the *World Economic Outlook* is available in full on the IMF's Internet site, *www.imf.org*. Accompanying it on the website is a larger compilation of data from the WEO database than in the report itself, consisting of files containing the series most frequently requested by readers. These files may be downloaded for use in a variety of software packages.

Inquiries about the content of the *World Economic Outlook* and the WEO database should be sent by mail, electronic mail, or telefax (telephone inquiries cannot be accepted) to:

World Economic Studies Division
Research Department
International Monetary Fund
700 19th Street, N.W.
Washington, D.C. 20431, U.S.A.
E-mail: weo@imf.org   Telefax: (202) 623-6343

PREFACE

This interim update of the IMF's latest regular reports on the *World Economic Outlook* (published in October 2001) provides a preliminary assessment of the global economic outlook and policies following the September 11 terrorist attacks. It reflects both the aftermath of the attacks and updated information on the global economy before September 11, much of which was unfavorable compared to what had been expected.

The analysis and projections contained in this report are integral elements of the IMF's surveillance of economic developments and policies in its member countries, developments in international financial markets, and the global economic system. The survey of prospects and policies is the product of a comprehensive interdepartmental review of world economic developments, which draws primarily on information the IMF staff gathered through its consultations with member countries. These consultations are carried out in particular by the IMF's area departments together with the Policy Development and Review Department, International Capital Markets Department, Monetary and Exchange Affairs Department, and the Fiscal Affairs Department.

The analysis in this report has been coordinated in the Research Department under the general direction of Kenneth Rogoff, Economic Counsellor and Director of Research. The project has been directed by David Robinson, Senior Advisor of the Research Department, together with Tamim Bayoumi, Division Chief, World Economic Studies Division.

Primary contributors to this report also include Maitland MacFarlan, Manmohan Kumar, Guy Meredith, and Torsten Sløk. Other contributors include Peter Breuer, Bankim Chadha, Michael DaCosta, Hali Edison, Thomas Helbling, Miguel Savastano, Silvia Sgherri, Phillip Swagel, Stephen Tokarick, and Cathy Wright. Bennett Sutton, Emily Conover, and Toh Kuan provided research assistance. Nicholas Dopuch, Mandy Hemmati, Yutong Li, Di Rao, and Anthony G. Turner processed the data and managed the computer systems. Sylvia Brescia, Viktória Kiss, Laura Leon, and Stephanie Whittaker were responsible for word processing. Jeff Hayden of the External Relations Department edited the manuscript and coordinated production of the publication.

The analysis has benefited from comments and suggestions by staff from other IMF departments, as well as by Executive Directors following their discussion of the report on December 11, 2001. However, both projections and policy considerations are those of the IMF staff and should not be attributed to Executive Directors or to their national authorities.

CHAPTER I

CONTAINING THE RISKS TO THE GLOBAL ECONOMY

The outlook for the global economy has deteriorated further in recent months, with growth continuing to weaken in almost all major regions of the world. The tragic events of September 11 and their aftermath, as well as evidence that the world economy was weaker than expected in the period before the attacks, contributed to a sharp deterioration in confidence across the globe, accompanied by a flight to quality in both mature and emerging markets, and a deterioration in emerging market financing conditions. As a result, prospects for global recovery have been set back significantly, and the IMF's projections for global growth have been marked down substantially since the October 2001 World Economic Outlook, by 0.2 percentage point to 2.4 percent in 2001, and by 1.1 percentage point to 2.4 percent in 2002 (Table 1.1 and Figure 1.1). While there are good reasons to expect a recovery to get under way in 2002, the outlook remains highly uncertain, and there is a significant possibility of a worse outcome, which could involve lower growth and external financing difficulties for many countries. Correspondingly, the primary challenge for policymakers is how best to support the prospects for recovery, and to limit the risks attendant on a deeper and longer downturn should that occur.

Since late 2000, growth has slowed sharply in almost all major regions of the world, accompanied by a marked decline in trade growth, significantly lower commodity prices, and deteriorating financing conditions in emerging markets (Figure 1.2). Before the terrorist attacks of September 11, there appeared a reasonable prospect of recovery in late 2001, although—as stressed in the October 2001 *World Economic Outlook*—the situation remained fragile and vulnerable to unexpected developments, and a significant danger of a deeper and more prolonged downturn remained. Data since that time indicate that the situation before the attacks was in fact weaker than earlier projected in many regions, including the United States, Europe, and Japan, as well as in a number of emerging market economies in Asia and Latin America.

The tragic events of September 11 exacerbated an already very difficult situation in the global economy. Following the attacks, consumer and business confidence have further weakened across the globe (Figure 1.3), and there was also a significant initial impact on demand and activity, particularly in the United States, although there are some signs that this is now beginning to stabilize. There was an initial generalized shift away from risky assets in both mature and emerging markets, including a substantial deterioration in financing conditions for emerging market countries. Over the ensuing period, however, financial markets have generally strengthened, reflected in a recovery in equity markets and most recently signs that the earlier flight to quality has begun to reverse (including a decline in high yield and many emerging market bond spreads to pre-September 11 levels). Movements in major exchange rates have on net been moderate, with the U.S. dollar appreciating modestly against the euro and the yen. As the outlook for global growth has weakened, commodity prices have fallen back further, especially for oil.

At present, the outlook is subject to great uncertainty, evident for example in the sharp increase in dispersion in private sector forecasts (Figure 1.4). It remains very difficult to judge how quickly confidence will rebound and how financial market conditions will develop, with

Table 1.1. Overview of the *World Economic Outlook* Projections
(Annual percent change unless otherwise noted)

	1999	2000	Current Projections		Difference from October 2001 Projections	
			2001	2002	2001	2002
World output	**3.6**	**4.7**	**2.4**	**2.4**	**−0.2**	**−1.1**
Advanced economies	3.3	3.9	1.1	0.8	−0.2	−1.3
Major advanced economies	3.0	3.5	1.0	0.6	−0.2	−1.3
United States	4.1	4.1	1.0	0.7	−0.3	−1.5
Japan	0.7	2.2	−0.4	−1.0	0.1	−1.3
Germany	1.8	3.0	0.5	0.7	−0.2	−1.1
France	3.0	3.5	2.1	1.3	0.1	−0.8
Italy	1.6	2.9	1.8	1.2	0.1	−0.8
United Kingdom	2.1	2.9	2.3	1.8	0.2	−0.6
Canada	5.1	4.4	1.4	0.8	−0.6	−1.4
Other advanced economies	4.9	5.2	1.5	1.9	−0.4	−1.3
Memorandum						
European Union	2.6	3.4	1.7	1.3	−0.1	−0.9
Euro area	2.6	3.4	1.5	1.2	−0.3	−1.0
Newly industrialized Asian economies	7.9	8.2	0.4	2.0	−0.6	−2.2
Developing countries	3.9	5.8	4.0	4.4	−0.4	−0.9
Africa	2.5	2.8	3.5	3.5	−0.3	−0.9
Developing Asia	6.2	6.8	5.6	5.6	−0.2	−0.5
China	7.1	8.0	7.3	6.8	−0.2	−0.3
India	6.8	6.0	4.4	5.2	−0.1	−0.5
ASEAN-4[1]	2.9	5.0	2.3	2.9	−0.1	−1.2
Middle East, Malta, and Turkey	1.1	5.9	1.8	3.9	−0.5	−0.9
Western Hemisphere	0.1	4.1	1.0	1.7	−0.7	−1.9
Brazil	0.5	4.4	1.8	2.0	−0.4	−1.4
Countries in transition	3.6	6.3	4.9	3.6	0.8	−0.4
Central and eastern Europe	2.0	3.8	3.0	3.2	−0.5	−1.0
Commonwealth of Independent States and Mongolia	4.6	7.8	6.1	3.9	1.7	−0.1
Russia	5.4	8.3	5.8	3.6	1.8	−0.4
Excluding Russia	2.8	6.8	6.8	4.6	1.5	0.5
World trade volume (goods and services)	**5.4**	**12.4**	**1.0**	**2.2**	**−1.8**	**−3.1**
Imports						
Advanced economies	7.7	11.5	−0.3	1.4	−2.0	−3.3
Developing countries	1.7	16.1	5.0	6.5	−1.4	−1.6
Countries in transition	−7.8	12.6	11.2	7.8	1.1	−0.2
Exports						
Advanced economies	5.2	11.6	−0.3	0.5	−2.1	−4.0
Developing countries	4.7	15.0	3.4	4.5	−1.6	−2.0
Countries in transition	0.2	16.3	7.8	6.4	0.7	−0.1
Commodity prices						
Oil[2]						
In SDRs	36.5	62.6	−11.2	−24.2	−9.8	−15.4
In U.S. dollars	37.5	56.9	−14.0	−23.7	−9.1	−15.1
Nonfuel (average based on world commodity export weights)						
In SDRs	−7.8	5.6	−2.3	1.1	−3.3	−3.2
In U.S. dollars	−7.0	1.8	−5.5	1.7	−2.8	−2.7
Consumer prices						
Advanced economies	1.4	2.3	2.3	1.3	−0.1	−0.4
Developing countries	6.8	5.9	6.0	5.3	0.1	0.2
Countries in transition	43.9	20.1	16.0	11.0	−0.3	0.3
Six-month London interbank offered rate (LIBOR, percent)						
On U.S. dollar deposits	5.5	6.6	3.8	2.8	−0.3	−0.9
On Japanese yen deposits	0.2	0.3	0.2	0.1	—	—
On euro deposits	3.0	4.6	4.1	2.9	−0.2	−1.0
Memorandum						
World growth based on market exchange rates	3.0	4.0	1.4	1.2	−0.2	−1.3

Note: Real effective exchange rates are assumed to remain constant at the levels prevailing during September 17–October 16, 2001.
[1]Includes Indonesia, Malaysia, the Philippines, and Thailand.
[2]Simple average of spot prices of U.K. Brent, Dubai, and West Texas Intermediate crude oil. The average price of oil in U.S. dollars a barrel was $28.21 in 2000, the assumed price is $24.20 in 2001, and $18.50 in 2002.

much continuing to depend on noneconomic factors, including the progress in the war against terrorism. Notwithstanding these uncertainties, there are a number of factors that will help to support recovery during 2002. First, policymakers have generally moved quickly to support activity. Monetary policy has been eased substantially in most major industrial countries, most notably the United States, where nominal short-term interest rates are now at a 40-year low, and an additional fiscal package is also under discussion. Together with the earlier macroeconomic stimulus already in the pipeline, these measures will provide significant support to activity in the course of 2002. Second, as discussed in Chapter II, oil prices have weakened sharply, reflecting weaker global demand and OPEC's continued difficulties in coordinating production cuts, particularly among non-OPEC producers. This will help support global activity, although there are clearly negative effects for oil producers, including a number of highly indebted countries. Third, the completion of ongoing inventory corrections will provide support to demand. Finally, the strengthening of economic fundamentals in many countries in recent years—notably lower inflation, generally improved fiscal positions, stronger external financial positions in many emerging market countries, especially Asia, and a shift toward more flexible exchange rates—has increased the room for policy maneuver and resilience to external shocks. Partly as a result, there appears to have been greater investor discrimination among countries than in some earlier episodes (see the Appendix to this chapter).

A particularly disturbing feature of the current slowdown is its synchronicity across nearly all regions (Figure 1.5), the most marked for at least two decades. To a considerable extent, this synchronicity is the result of common shocks, including the increase in oil prices and the bursting of the information technology (IT) bubble, both of which had a worldwide impact. Increased international linkages, particularly in the financial and corporate sectors, have played

Figure 1.1. Global Indicators[1]
(Annual percent change unless otherwise noted)

Global growth is projected to slow markedly in 2001–02, while inflation remains subdued.

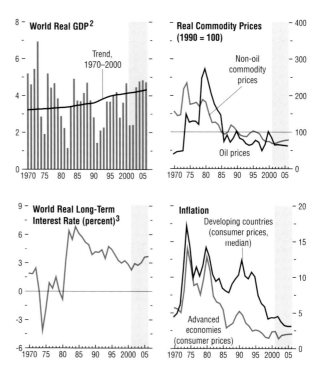

[1]Shaded areas indicate IMF staff projections. Aggregates are computed on the basis of purchasing-power-parity weights unless otherwise indicated.
[2]Average growth rates for individual countries, aggregated using purchasing-power-parity weights; these shift over time in favor of faster growing countries, giving the line an upward trend.
[3]GDP-weighted average of the 10-year (or nearest maturity) government bond yields less inflation rates for the United States, Japan, Germany, France, Italy, the United Kingdom, and Canada. Excluding Italy prior to 1972.

a role—a trend that is likely to continue. The synchronicity of the downturn may also reflect delays in implementing structural reforms, notably in Japan and the euro area, which have meant that these countries have been less well placed to take up the slack when the long expansion in the United States came to an end.

The IMF's projections now envisage a deeper and more prolonged global slowdown than foreseen in the October 2001 *World Economic Outlook* (where the forecast was completed before the September 11 events). Global GDP growth is now projected at 2.4 percent in 2001, and is expected to remain at about that level in 2002 (a reduction of about 1 percentage point from the forecast made prior to the attacks).[1] However, with the recovery picking up during 2002 as the positive impact of the factors described above begins to be felt, global growth for 2003 as a whole would be expected to bounce back strongly:

- Among the industrial economies, the recession in the *United States* is expected to be followed by a recovery during 2002 as the positive factors noted above take effect. *Canada* is expected to follow a similar pattern, reflecting its close integration with the United States. Projections for the *euro area* have been reduced markedly, especially for *Germany*, reflecting both the weaker-than-expected situation before the September 11 attacks as well as the aftermath. The outlook for *Japan* has become increasingly worrying, and the economy is now expected to experience two consecutive years of contraction for the first time in the postwar period, and the situation in the banking system is of increasing concern.
- Among emerging market countries, the effects of recent events vary widely, depending on the structure of the economy and the strength of economic fundamentals. The

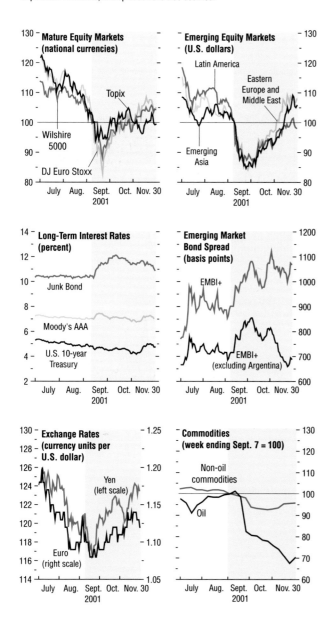

Figure 1.2. Selected Financial Market Indicators
(September 10, 2001 = 100 unless otherwise noted)

Financial markets have generally recovered from initial losses following the September 11 attacks, and spreads have also declined.

Sources: Bloomberg Financial Markets, LP; and IMF staff estimates.

---

[1]Evaluated using weights based on market exchange rates, rather than purchasing power parity weights used in the *World Economic Outlook*, global growth would be 1.4 percent in 2001 and 1.2 percent in 2002.

impact has been particularly heavy in *Latin America*, where a number of countries may be affected by the deterioration in external financing conditions, the precarious situation in *Argentina*, weaker external demand, including the marked downturn in tourism, and lower commodity prices, especially oil. In *emerging Asia*, growth is expected to remain reasonably robust in *China* and to a lesser extent *India*, which are less exposed to external developments; elsewhere, notwithstanding additional policy stimulus and the generally beneficial effect of lower oil prices and lower global interest rates, growth has been marked down sharply owing to weakening external demand and the further deterioration in the IT sector. In the *Middle East*, growth will be adversely affected by lower oil prices and production, and in some cases weaker remittances and tourism revenues. In *Turkey*, the outlook has been affected by weaker external demand, especially for tourist services, and more difficult financing conditions. In contrast, the impact of recent events in the *Commonwealth of Independent States* is expected to be modest, buoyed by strong domestic demand in *Russia*. Growth in *central and eastern Europe* is also expected to remain reasonably resilient, owing mainly to the benefits of lower oil prices and supportive policies.

- The poorest countries are being hurt by weaker external demand and falling commodity prices, with oil exporters particularly affected. Nonfuel commodity exporters will also be affected by further weakness in already depressed prices, especially for agricultural commodities, although for some the benefits from lower oil prices will limit the increase in external financing requirements. On the macroeconomic side, while the outlook for individual countries varies widely, growth is projected to be relatively well sustained for the group as a whole. However, this may understate the impact on poverty, as lower prices for agricultural goods will hurt rural areas, where most of

Figure 1.3 Selected European Union Countries, Japan, and United States: Indicators of Consumer and Business Confidence[1]

Business and consumer confidence have continued to weaken across the globe since September 11.

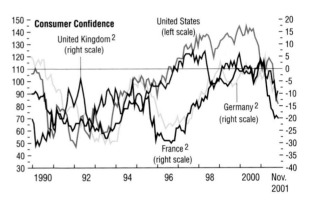

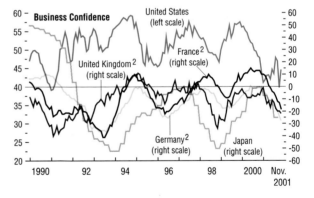

Sources: Consumer confidence for the United States, the Conference Board; for European countries, the European Commission. Business confidence for the United States, the U.S. Department of Commerce, Purchasing Managers Composite Diffusion Index; for European countries, the European Commission; and for Japan, Bank of Japan.

[1]Indicators are not comparable across countries.
[2]Percent of respondents expecting an improvement in their situation minus percent expecting a deterioration.

Figure 1.4. Private Sector Forecasts
(Percent)

Private sector forecasts have been revised downwards substantially since the September 11 attacks, and their dispersion has increased significantly—as was the case during the run up to the Gulf War.

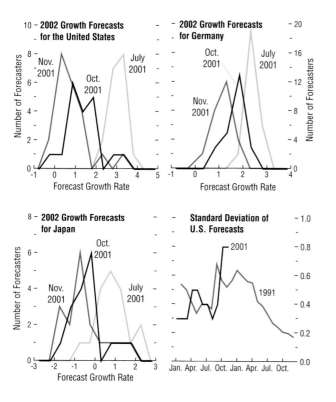

Source: Consensus Economics, Inc.

the poor live, while the benefits of lower oil prices tend to accrue in urban areas.

As already noted, there are unusually large uncertainties and risks to the forecast. With substantial policy stimulus in the pipeline, particularly in the United States, faster-than-expected progress in the war on terrorism in Afghanistan, and possible downside risks to oil prices, there is a possibility that recovery in 2002 could come more rapidly than presently expected. This outturn also appears to be expected in financial markets given the recovery in equity markets, and the steepening of yield curves. Were that to occur, policymakers would need to begin to withdraw a portion of the stimulus that is now in the pipeline. However, given the already difficult situation for the global economy, and the large costs associated with a deeper slowdown, the possibility of a worse outcome remains the major policy issue at the current juncture. There are four interlinked areas of risk (whose implications for the outlook are discussed in more detail in Chapter III):

- *Confidence and activity in the United States may pick up more slowly than currently expected.* For instance, the effects of the terrorist attacks themselves may prove more prolonged; or recovery may be more severely hampered by the imbalances accumulated in the past, including overinvestment, particularly in the IT sector, and consumers' relatively high indebtedness.[2] In addition, there are also downside risks to activity in the *other major currency areas*. With no major region providing substantive support to activity, further weakness in any one area would reinforce the already synchronized downturn. This could result in a renewed withdrawal from risk taking in financial markets, as well as even lower commodity prices, both of which would adversely affect developing countries in general and emerging market economies in particular.

---

[2]See "Alternative Scenarios—How Might Medium-Term Productivity Growth Affect the Short-Term Outlook," Chapter I, Appendix II of the October 2001 *World Economic Outlook.*

- *The outlook for many emerging market countries will continue to depend on developments in global risk aversion and the period for which bond issuance is largely limited to only high grade borrowers, as well as the extent of the squeeze generated by refinancing pressures in the meantime.* While the recent decline in spreads is encouraging, market access for many countries remains limited. Financing pressures could become significantly larger and more widespread if the global outlook deteriorates further, or the resolution of a credit event in a major emerging market proves disorderly and prolongs or exacerbates difficult market conditions.

- *The imbalances in the global economy—including the large U.S. current account deficit and surpluses elsewhere, the apparent overvaluation of the U.S. dollar, and richly valued equity markets by historical standards—remain an important source of risk.* As discussed in Chapter II, mature equity markets appear to be pricing in a relatively rapid recovery—although they remain well below their levels in March, when the U.S. recession began—and currency options market data suggest that expectations of a sharp depreciation in the U.S. dollar have not increased since the attack. However, it remains unclear whether asset markets have fully priced in the deterioration in corporate credit quality and earnings prospects that has occurred thus far. An abrupt adjustment remains possible, particularly if the global growth outlook were to prove worse than expected, especially given the recent reduction in market liquidity—notably in the markets for credit swaps and derivatives—and the financial difficulties faced by some major market participants, including insurance companies.

- *Slowing growth and a further flight to quality in financial markets would increase pressure on corporate and financial sectors across the globe.* This is of particular concern in Japan, where banks are highly exposed to developments in equity and bond markets, but may also

Figure 1.5. Global Output, Industrial Production, and Trade Growth
(Percent change from four quarters earlier)

Growth in output and industrial production has weakened in almost every region of the globe, accompanied by a sharp slowdown in the growth of trade flows.

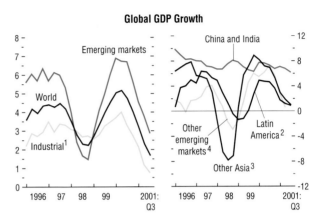

Global GDP Growth

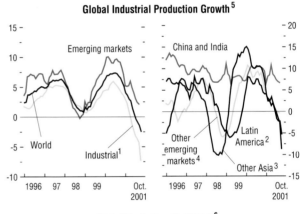

Global Industrial Production Growth[5]

Global Trade Growth (SDRs)[6]

Sources: Central banks and ministries of finance; and European Central Bank *Monthly Bulletin.*
[1]Canada, Euro area, Japan, United Kingdom, and United States.
[2]Argentina, Brazil, Chile, Colombia, Mexico, Peru, and Venezuela.
[3]Hong Kong SAR, Indonesia, Korea, Malaysia, Philippines, Singapore, Taiwan Province of China, and Thailand.
[4]Czech Republic, Hungary, Israel, Poland, Russia, Turkey, Pakistan, and South Africa.
[5]Twelve-month percent change of three-month moving average.
[6]Defined as exports plus imports of the relevant region. Twelve-month percent change of three-month moving average.

become more important in other countries in Asia and Latin America.

Against this background, the primary challenge faced by policymakers is how best to support the prospects for recovery and to limit the risks attendant on a deeper and longer recession. In doing so, a variety of factors need to be taken into account. First, given the synchronicity of the slowdown, policies in both industrial and developing countries must be viewed in a global perspective to ensure that there is adequate global demand. Second, the nature of the policy response is affected by the uncertainty in the outlook, and—with inflationary pressures across the globe increasingly subdued—the relatively higher costs associated with a weaker-than-projected outlook (Box 1.1). Finally, account also needs to be taken of existing fiscal frameworks, like the Stability and Growth Pact in the euro area, and country specific constraints, like Japan's already very high fiscal deficit and government debt.

Given the degree of uncertainty and the constraints on fiscal policies in a number of countries, monetary policy—the most flexible instrument—has appropriately played the primary role to date. Nonetheless, fiscal policy should also play a role, particularly through the operation of the automatic stabilizers, and it will be important that countries do not interpret their individual constraints too rigidly, particularly if the situation deteriorates further. From a global perspective, there are two potential concerns. First, policy easing in the United States could exacerbate already large imbalances, including the large external current account deficit. While this should not constrain short-term macroeconomic policies in present circumstances, policies over the medium term—both in the United States and elsewhere—must be consistent with reducing those imbalances. Second, given the increasingly difficult external environment, many emerging market countries have been forced to restrain domestic demand to maintain the confidence of international investors. The aggregate effect is of partic-

ular importance in certain regions, but also adds a further downward impulse to global demand, which—while presently moderate from a global perspective[3]—could become larger if the situation were to deteriorate further.

Against this background, there is a need for a coordinated and collaborative policy response by the international community.[4] In industrial countries, which remain the key engines of growth in the world economy, economic policies should help to sustain demand, especially given the synchronized nature of the slowdown. To date, monetary policy has appropriately been eased, and further room remains if necessary, including through a more aggressive approach to monetary easing in Japan. On the fiscal side, additional stimulus presently under consideration in the United States could be helpful if implemented sufficiently rapidly, while demand is still weak. It should be carefully designed to shore up consumer confidence and boost activity in the short run, without exacerbating medium-term fiscal pressures (see Box 3.2). In Europe, the automatic stabilizers should be allowed to operate in full, while in Japan the second supplementary budget will go a significant way toward avoiding a withdrawal of stimulus in 2002, and thereby reducing downside risks to activity. Structural reforms in Japan and Europe remain crucial, both to improve growth potential and boost confidence, and to help reduce global imbalances over the longer term.

In developing and emerging markets, there is considerably less room for policy maneuver, although where it exists it should be used. From the domestic policy perspective, early adjustment where necessary remains critical, accompanied by structural reforms—particularly of financial and corporate sectors—to help reduce vulnerability. For its part, the international community should provide strong support for such efforts, both through the international financial institutions and other channels. Particularly if the global situation were to deteriorate further, due attention

[3]Net debtor developing countries account for 18 percent of global trade.
[4]As noted by the IMF's Managing Director (Köhler, 2001).

Box 1.1. Policymaking Under Uncertainty

An important problem faced by policymakers is uncertainty, both about the future economic environment and the effects of policies themselves. In setting instruments, policymakers must accept that desired outcomes will not, in general, be realized due to unanticipated factors. Furthermore, the degree of uncertainty is likely to change over time. For instance, a banking crisis could increase uncertainty about the effectiveness of monetary policy. Of more immediate relevance, the September 11 terrorist attacks have not only led to lower growth forecasts, but also increased the variance around these forecasts. Should policymakers take uncertainty into account in setting instruments? If so, what is the appropriate response to heightened uncertainty?

Conceptually, uncertainty matters in the presence of "nonlinearities" in the costs of deviating from desired outcomes. The first panel in the figure provides a hypothetical example of a nonlinear relationship between a social welfare index and a policy target. Given uncertainty, the desired level of the target variable cannot be systematically attained, and social welfare will average less than its maximum value. Furthermore, social welfare will fall as the variance of outcomes for the target variable rises. This relationship forms the basis of the prescription that policies should, in general, "underreact" to changes in the economic environment when their effects are uncertain: the benefit of moving the expected value for the objective closer to its optimal level must be traded off against creating greater volatility in the objective due to uncertainty regarding the effects of policies.[1]

Is there also a case for *amplifying* the response? The latter approach can be justified when the costs of deviating from a desired outcome are "asymmetric" and the degree of uncertainty changes. The second panel in the figure illustrates a relationship where the loss in social welfare when the target variable is below its opti-

[1]Relative to the response required to move the expected value for the target variable back to its original level. See Brainard (1967).

Policy Targets and Welfare Functions

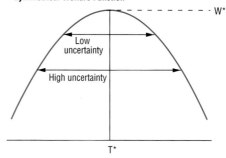

Symmetrical Welfare Function[1]

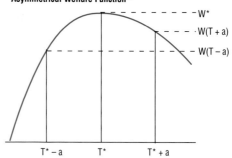

Asymmetrical Welfare Function[2]

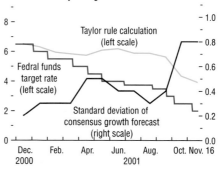

U.S. Monetary Easing

Sources: Bloomberg Financial Markets, LP; Consensus Forecast; and IMF staff estimates.
[1]Social welfare is maximized at W* when the policy target is at T*. But T* cannot be hit with certainty. As the dispersion of outcomes around T* increases, the average level of W decreases.
[2]Equal-sized deviations in the policy target around T* have different effects on welfare—exceeding the target is less costly than falling short of it. Policies should aim for a level of T that exceeds T*. This difference will rise as the volatility of T increases.

Box 1.1 *(concluded)*

mal level is greater than when it exceeds it. An example of why such an asymmetry might exist involves the zero lower bound for nominal interest rates. When inflation is initially low, a negative output shock would increase the chances of hitting this lower bound, at which point conventional monetary instruments would become ineffective at stimulating demand. Given such an asymmetry, expected social welfare is raised when policymakers aim for a level of the target that exceeds its optimal value in the absence of uncertainty, with a gap that increases as uncertainty rises.

The recent terrorist attacks have both lowered growth forecasts and increased uncertainty around them. Assuming the "optimal" level of real growth in the absence of uncertainty is unchanged,[2] how should policies respond? In the presence of uncertainty about the effects of policies, the traditional argument calls for easing by less than needed to restore expected growth to its initial level. With increased uncertainty around the growth forecast and greater costs to low versus high outcomes, however, there is an argument for easing by more than this amount.

The relative weight of these arguments depends on the degree of uncertainty in the effects of policies compared with differences in the costs of low versus high outcomes. This balance will vary over time and across countries. In the United States, the success of monetary authorities in conducting policy in recent years suggests that policy effects have been relatively predictable. In addition, enhanced credibility has reduced the risk that temporary economic overheating could destabilize inflation expectations.

[2]This characterization, of course, abstracts from many real world policy considerations.

On the downside, the abrupt drop in growth forecasts, weakening confidence, and the reversal of earlier price shocks raises deflationary risks. In this environment, it seems natural to attach greater weight to the risks of weaker rather than stronger growth, suggesting a relatively strong response. This seems consistent with the recent behavior of the U.S. Federal Reserve. As shown in the third panel, the Federal Reserve funds target rate has been lowered by more since the end of 2000 than a simple "Taylor-rule" calculation would indicate.[3] At the same time, uncertainty about the forecast has risen, as indicated by the rise in the standard deviation of the Consensus growth forecast for 2002.

Another issue concerns the choice of policy instrument—that is, monetary or fiscal policy. Monetary policy is the standard tool of choice for dealing with cyclical fluctuations, and can be implemented more quickly and flexibly than fiscal policy. The effects of fiscal policy, however, may be felt sooner and more predictably than those of monetary policy. Theoretically, uncertainty creates a case for using multiple instruments to achieve a single target, as smaller movements in several instruments create less uncertainty than a large movement in one instrument. On balance, it seems plausible that the primary emphasis should remain on monetary policy, with automatic fiscal stabilizers playing a supportive role, although the case for discretionary fiscal measures increases as uncertainty rises.

[3]The Taylor rule is based on changes in the Consensus growth and inflation forecasts. The standard parameter values of $1\frac{1}{2}$ and $\frac{1}{2}$ are applied to cumulative revisions to the monthly forecasts of inflation and output (respectively) for 2001 and 2002.

will need to be paid to the appropriate mix between adjustment and financing. For the poorest countries, additional concessional financing may be required. In this connection a rapid increase in official development assistance toward the U.N. target takes on additional urgency.

Finally, there remains an important question as to the potential long-term impact of increased security concerns on economic activity. The main channel through which productive potential could be affected is through higher "transactions" costs associated with greater uncertainty—

Table 1.2. The Channels of Contagion or Spillovers in Selected Crises

	Bilateral Trade with Initially Affected Country[1]	Trade with a Common Third Party[2]	Common Lender[3]	Level of Market Liquidity[4]	Global Reduction in Appetite for Risk[5]
Mexico, December 1994					
Argentina	—	Low	Yes, little exposure	Low	Moderate decline in risk
Brazil	—	Low	Yes, little exposure	High	appetite in January 1995.
Thailand, July 1997					
Hong Kong SAR	—	Low	No	High	Modest decline in risk
Indonesia	—	Low	Yes, moderate exposure	Low	appetite in May 1997, but
Malaysia	Low	High	Yes, moderate exposure	Moderate	not sustained.
Philippines	Low	Moderate	No	Low	
South Korea	—	Moderate	Yes, high exposure	Moderate	
Russia, August 1998					
Brazil	—	—	No	High	Marked decline in risk
Hong Kong SAR	—	—	No	High	appetite in August and
Mexico	—	—	No	Moderate/high	September.

Sources: IMF (2001); Kaminsky and Reinhart (2000); Kumar and Persaud (2001); and Glick, and Rose, 1999.
[1]Exposure through bilateral trade is measured by the share of the country's total exports destined to the initial crisis country.
[2]Trade with a common third party in the same commodities is measured as the percent of total exports competing with the top exports of initial crisis country.
[3]For a discussion of how Bank of International Settlements data can be used to identify common bank lender clusters, see Kaminsky and Reinhart (2000). For bonds, see J.P. Morgan's EMBI+ weights.
[4]Market liquidity is roughly proxied by the country's representation (its share) in the global mutual funds' emerging market portfolio. High, moderate, and low classifications are comparisons with respect to other emerging markets.
[5]For a description of the methodology used to estimate risk appetite, see Kumar and Persaud (2001).

such as greater spending on security; higher levels of inventories; lower investor appetite for risk; and a shift away from globalization. While these costs are real, it is impossible to estimate their size with any certainty at this stage. As discussed in Chapter II, while there will be a short-term impact on productivity, such costs would have to be both large and long lived to have a significant impact on medium- and long-term growth trends. Nonetheless, this reinforces the need to press forward with structural and other reforms designed to increase long-run productive potential. The agreement reached at the World Trade Organization meetings in Doha in November to launch a new trade round is therefore of particular importance and could contribute substantially to global economic growth over the medium term.

Appendix: Contagion and Its Causes

The likelihood of a default on loans in Argentina has sparked considerable interest in the prospects for contagion in emerging markets. Most often, contagion is defined as excess comovements in asset prices or returns that cannot be explained by changes in fundamentals. Asset prices across countries may show a high degree of comovement when markets react to changes in common fundamentals, such as international interest rates or oil prices. Such comovement, however, would typically not be viewed as contagion. Comovement may also arise if significant cross-country trade or financial linkages are present—some of these linkages may be very difficult to quantify. Finally, herding behavior—for rational or irrational reasons— may also give rise to large spikes in cross-country correlation of asset returns.

What are the channels through which contagion takes place? While spillovers through trade have been shown to be statistically significant, trade effects tend to be gradual and protracted (see, for instance, Glick and Rose, 1999). As shown in Table 1.2, in the major contagion episodes, the countries that suffered the most had minimal trade linkages;[5] financial sector links, through common ownership of emerging markets financial assets, such as bonds, loans or

[5]The episodes are the Mexican peso crisis of December 1994; the Asian crisis that began with the devaluation of the Thai baht in 1997; and the Russian–Long Term Capital Management (LTCM) crisis of August 1998.

Figure 1.6. Average Cross-Correlation of Emerging Debt Markets

Recent crises have not spurred the broad based sell-offs witnessed in earlier crises.

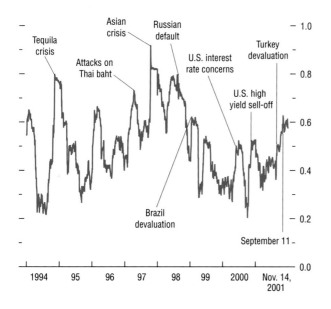

Source: IMF, *Emerging Markets Financing.*

equity, were significantly more important. For example, common bank lenders were an important vehicle of contagion in the Asian crisis. Investors' appetites for risk may also diminish in times of market stress and increased uncertainty, as in the Russian Crisis–Long Term Capital Management episode and more recently after the September 11 terrorist attacks (see Kumar and Persaud, 2001).

A common methodology for *measuring financial contagion* is to examine the comovement of country asset returns, as shown in Figure 1.6.[6] The Figure reports the average (unweighted mean) *cross correlation* of daily returns of the key constituent countries of the EMBI+ benchmark index since its inception at the beginning of 1994 (a 50-day window is used). A high average cross correlation indicates investors are either broadly buying or selling across all emerging market credits. Periods of broad-based selling or buying of emerging markets are consistent with the factors listed earlier, including common external shocks and lack of investor discrimination.

There are several notable features of the Figure:

- The average cross correlation has always been positive, with a mean value during 1994–2000 of 0.51, suggesting a substantial tendency for returns on individual countries to move together. The high mean cross correlation over the sample reflects large spikes associated with the major emerging market crises: the Tequila crisis in early 1995 (when the average cross correlation reached 0.8); the attacks on the Thai baht in early May 1997 (0.7); the October 1997 Asian Crisis (0.9); and the Russian default (0.8).
- Individual country returns have tended to move together during bad times, but considerably less so during market rallies. This suggests less investor discrimination during sell-offs. This is consistent with the "crossover" nature of the investor base, which tends to head for its home markets in the face of bad

[6]For a more detailed discussion on the measure, see IMF (2001).

news. The asymmetry may also owe to leveraged position taking, where losses prompt margin calls and broad-based liquidation across the asset class, but gains do not.

- The average cross correlation has fallen off substantially since the crises of 1997–98. At the time of the floating of the Brazilian real in January 1999, for example, the peak occurred around 0.6, a level that has not been revisited until the aftermath of September 11. Several factors have played a role in reducing the extent of contagion during more recent episodes of market turbulence. First, the leverage in the investor base has declined. The need for across-the-board liquidations in response to margin calls have, therefore, been fewer. Second, the upgrade of some countries in the EMBI+—such as Mexico—to investment grade has increased the diversity of the overall investor base, as the proportion of high-grade investors has gone up, which should result in divergent behavior. Furthermore, the fundamentals in some of the key emerging market countries have improved, leaving them in a better position to cope with any economic fallout that may arise owing to contagion.

Since 1998 there has not been a credit event in a major emerging market. It remains an open question as to how much contagion there would be if such an event were to actually take place. The heightened credit concerns have come at a time of much lower exuberance in emerging markets. Net emerging markets fundraising on international capital markets, for example, was $196 billion in 1997—the year of the Asian Crisis; in 2000, at $98 billion, it was still only half its previous peak. The global slowdown has long been anticipated, drawing capital up the credit spectrum and away from higher risk asset classes, including emerging markets. In the case of Argentina, investor concerns have been building for some time, thereby allowing dedicated investors to take underweight positions in Argentina and Brazil and have, since late last year, overweighted Mexico and Russia. This is in sharp contrast to previous crisis episodes, where

there was a mass exit out of the asset class. The increased investor discrimination largely owes to the rising importance of dedicated and local investors in emerging debt markets. Since local investors typically hold only their own country's external debt, for regulatory or home-bias reasons, they are unlikely to be a channel for spillovers. The major episodes of contagion in emerging markets shared the element of surprise. Financial markets react strongly to unanticipated events. While the devaluation of the ruble may have been anticipated, the default on debt was not.

In conclusion, the current environment confronting emerging markets and changes in the investor base and positioning help explain the limited broad-based contagion in emerging markets so far and suggest the potential for future contagion is less than it was in the past. But past episodes of contagion were associated with discrete events and, therefore, the potential for contagion, were a credit event to occur in one of the major emerging markets, remains.

References

Brainard, William, 1967, "Uncertainty and Effectiveness of Policy," *American Economic Review*, Vol. 57 (May).

Glick, Reuven, and Andrew K. Rose, 1999, "Contagion and Trade: Why Are Currency Crises Regional?" *Journal of International Money and Finance*, Vol. 18 (August), pp. 603–17.

IMF, 2001, *Emerging Market Financing*, International Monetary Fund (various issues). Available on the Internet at *www.imf.org/external/pubs/ft/emf/index.htm*

Kaminsky, Graciela, and Carmen Reinhart, 2000, "On Crises, Contagion, and Confusion," *Journal of International Economics*, Vol. 51 (June), pp. 145–68.

Köhler, Horst, 2001, Statement of the Managing Director on the Situation of the World Economy and the Fund Response, IMF News Brief No. 01/98, October 5. Also available on the Internet at *www.imf.org/external/np/sec/nb/2001/nb0198.htm*

Kumar, Manmohan S., and Avinash Persaud, 2001, "Pure Contagion and Investors' Shifting Risk Appetite: Analytical Issues and Empirical Evidence," IMF Working Paper Series No. 01/134 (Washington: International Monetary Fund).

CHAPTER II

HOW HAS SEPTEMBER 11 INFLUENCED THE GLOBAL ECONOMY?

This Chapter analyzes the channels through which the terrorist attacks on September 11 could affect the global economy, and hence the underlying issues that have helped to mold the forecast and policy advice. The multiplicity of the channels—ranging from the direct loss of life and property to the impact on commodity markets—reflects the complex web of relationships that make up the world economy.

Before examining the channels in more detail it is useful to review the economic environment in which the terrorist attacks occurred. The global slowdown that had started most prominently in the United States in 2000 had, by mid-2001, become a synchronized downturn across almost all major regions of the world. This left the global economy particularly vulnerable to a negative impulse through, among other things, an erosion of the financial position of consumers, corporations, and governments. Such difficult times are also those in which sentiment can be particularly affected by unexpected negative shocks, leading to relatively abrupt reductions in private spending. The room for policy maneuver may have also been constrained by earlier policy easing and, particularly in emerging market economies dependent on external financing, lower investor appetite for risk. In short, the underlying impact of the terrorist attacks was probably magnified by the particular circumstances in which it occurred.

Bearing this in mind, the chapter focuses on four relatively distinct channels through which the attacks affect the global macroeconomic situation in the short term:

- *The destruction of life and property.* This includes the tragic loss of human life, the costs of replacing the buildings and equipment destroyed in the attack, and the disruption of activities in the immediate after-math of September 11. Also included are the somewhat longer-term disruptions to specific industries, most notably to the global airline industry and related services, such as hotels, local transportation, tourism, civilian aircraft manufacture, and restaurants, as well as the postal service in the wake of the anthrax scare in the United States.

- *The confidence channel.* An unexpected event of the magnitude of the September 11 attacks alters the assessment of economic risks by both consumers and businesses in a negative way. The resulting deterioration in confidence about the future can reduce the incentive to spend as opposed to save, a process that can spread through the economy and the rest of the world through normal business cycle and trade channels.

- *Financial market responses.* By their nature, financial instruments involve commitments across time, and thus are affected by perceptions of the future. For example, equity and bond markets trade securities involving future dividend or coupon payments by corporations or governments. In addition, derivative markets can provide information about the level of uncertainty in traded markets, an issue of particular interest after such an unexpected event as the terrorist attack. The initial generalized fall in asset prices has now been reversed, although borrowing costs for riskier borrowers remain high.

- *Commodity markets.* Slowing activity will reduce the demand for commodities and other goods sold in similar markets, such as computer chips, while initial concerns that supply might also be disrupted (most notably in the oil market) have not thus far transpired. As a result, commodities prices (particularly for oil) have weakened sharply, reducing the impact of the fall in aggregate demand in industrial countries by transferring part of these losses to commodity producers through the terms of trade.

The importance of the channels varies by country. For the major industrial countries, the main impact is likely to depend primarily on the fall in demand generated by the loss in confidence about the economy and its impact on output, together with the direct effect on some industries. This reaction is most notable in the United States. Slowing external demand (including tourism) is the major factor for many emerging market economies, particularly in Asia, central America, and the Caribbean, while elsewhere in Latin America the main channel is likely to be through a flight to quality in financial markets, which increases the cost of borrowing for emerging markets, as they are seen as relatively risky borrowers. Finally, both the trade and financial channels will matter for central Europe and Russia. For other developing countries, including many of the poorest, the main impact is likely to come through commodity markets.

There is also the question of whether the attacks are likely to have a long-term impact on long-term productive potential around the world by raising the costs of transactions through, for example, significantly increased security and higher insurance premiums, as discussed in Box 2.1. While any assessment of the long-term impact is inevitably speculative at this stage, and views differ markedly, two points are worth highlighting:

- *The impact will probably not be large in comparison to existing growth trends.* Over the last decade, real GDP has been rising at a rate of some 2¾ percent a year in the advanced economies and double that in developing countries. If the impact on the level of potential output were relatively sizable, say 1 percent of GDP, its impact on medium-term growth would be significantly smaller than current estimates of the impact of information technology on U.S. growth since the mid-1990s, a matter of continuing contro-

versy given the natural variation in growth trends due to cyclical events. As such, the shock is probably best characterized as a temporary disturbance.

- *Real GDP (the conventional measure of output) is a good cyclical indicator of the state of the economy, but in current circumstances may overstate economic welfare.* In particular, the increased awareness of the possibility of terrorist actions reduces people's welfare through great concern about security, but has no impact on real GDP. By contrast, the resulting increases in demand for security services to relieve these concerns are counted in real GDP.

Direct Impact of the Attacks

Like all major disasters, natural or manmade, the terrorist attacks of September 11 resulted in a tragic loss of life and destruction of property, as well as a short-term disruption of activity more generally. In addition, because of the size and premeditated nature of the attack, there are likely to be more lasting effects in some industries, most notably airlines, civilian aircraft manufacture, hotels, insurance, leisure activities, and the postal service (taking into account the subsequent anthrax attack). The analysis indicates that while the human toll and property damage are likely to have a limited macroeconomic impact, the short-term losses through specific industries could be significant.

The U.S. National Income and Product Accounts (NIPA) estimate the losses to property from the September 11 attack at about $16 billion, just over 0.15 percent of annual GDP and an even smaller percentage of the U.S. capital stock—see Table 2.1 (U.S. Bureau of Economic Analysis 2001a, b). The property damage is somewhat smaller than from the earthquake in Northridge, California in early 1994 and Hurricane Andrew in 1992. In addition, the horrific loss of life and injuries are estimated to lead to other insurance costs of approximately $5 billion (0.5 percent of annual GDP, excluding the recent anthrax attack through the postal

Table 2.1. Direct Costs of September 11 Attacks
(Billions of U.S. dollars)

Loss	Cost
Structures, Equipment, and Software	
Private	14.0
State and local government[1]	1.5
Federal government	0.7
Subtotal	16.2
Other Insurance Losses	
Life and related costs	2.6
Workers compensation	1.8
Homeowners and other	0.6
General government	0.2
Subtotal	5.2
Total	**21.4**

Source: U.S. Bureau of Econnomic Analysis (2001a, b).
[1]Largely NYC subways.

news (TV viewership surged by almost half immediately after the attacks) and some avoided public places (average shopping mall traffic fell by 5 percent or more). Somewhat smaller effects appear to have occurred elsewhere in the world. In addition, the closure of U.S. airports for four days was a blow to airlines in the United States and elsewhere, with knock-on effects on related industries. The closure of the U.S. stock exchanges for four days and other financial disruption (see Box 2.2) reduced revenues, but higher volume thereafter probably largely offset these losses. The overall impact on GDP was small, about 0.1 percent of monthly GDP.[2]

Looking beyond the short term, the fact that the attack was premeditated and therefore could be repeated has had a significant impact on three specific areas of activity—airlines and other industries associated with travel, postal services, and insurance. In most cases the effects are largest in the United States and for small countries particularly specialized in certain industries:

- *Airlines.* In the United States, the airline industry was already in a weak financial position before the attacks, with rising debt ratios and falling returns on investment. Even with cutbacks in service of the order of 20 percent and significant government support, airline passenger traffic has apparently remained below normal, 100,000 layoffs have been announced, and employment in October and November fell by 81,000 (almost 8 percent). These problems extend to other countries, as the near bankruptcy of Swissair followed by the actual bankruptcy of the Belgian airline Sabena illustrate. Equity valuations compared to the overall market illustrate these difficulties (Figure 2.1). The U.S. airline sector has lost around 20 percent of its relative value since

system), although the timing of these payouts is difficult to determine.[1] Total costs are hence around ¼ percent of annual GDP.

Even including the injury costs, the damage inflicted by Japan's Kobe earthquake in 1995—which had little impact on the path of the Japanese economy in either the short or longer term—was much greater than that caused by the September 11 attacks in both absolute terms and relative to GDP (see Box 1.3 of the October 2001 *World Economic Outlook*). One reason that such disasters have a smaller macroeconomic impact is that they boost demand in a number of sectors, most notably construction, and, in the case of September 11, defense spending. In addition, insurance claims are transfers from one person to another and hence do not reduce overall incomes—indeed, as many of the policies were reinsured abroad, there will be a net inflow to the United States estimated to be $11 billion (0.1 percent of GDP).

The attacks also resulted in a series of temporary disruptions to the complex web of transactions that make up a modern economy. In the United States, consumption fell significantly in September as people followed the

[1]The direct impact on human capital will be miniscule given the size of the U.S. labor force of 140 million.
[2]NIPA estimates are that in the third quarter consumer spending fell by $0.7 billion and temporary layoffs lowered wages by $3.3 billion, partially offset by $0.8 billion in additional pay for emergency service workers (all figures quarterly at annualized rates).

September 10, while in Europe and Japan the reduction is around 15 percent.

- *Other service industries* have also been badly affected, such as hotels, tourism, car hire, travel agents, restaurants, and civilian aircraft manufacturers, while postal use fell after recent anthrax scares. For example, hotels have reported higher vacancy rates, and employment in the sector as a whole in the United States fell by 58,000 (about 3 percent) in October and November. Tourism has been particularly affected in regions of the world dependent on foreign visitors, such as the Caribbean (see Chapter III, Box 3.3), parts of the Middle East, and portions of Asia. Relative equity values for hotels and leisure facilities are off by around 15 percent in the United States and Europe, although they have gained slightly in Japan, possibly reflecting the more limited need for air travel.

- *Insurance.* The industry will be affected by large claims resulting from the attacks, but gain from heightened uncertainty and interest in security. Anecdotal evidence largely from the United States indicates that insurers have been able to raise premiums, while it remains unclear how far governments will get involved in covering losses from terrorism and war. The market assessment is that the benefits of higher premiums will dominate, as relative equity prices for insurance brokers (and the reinsurance subsector that was particularly affected by the attack) have risen by around 10 percent in the United States and in Europe.

Significant disruption in these sectors could have an impact on real GDP in the short term. In the United States, for example, air travel, hotels, and leisure activities comprise about 2¾ percent of GDP, so a temporary 20 percent fall in such activities would reduce output by around ½ percent, although this would be partially offset by increases in demand for substitute products—less air travel may well raise the demand for other forms of communication, such as railroads and telephone calls.

Figure 2.1. Stock Market Indices by Industry
(September 10, 2001 = 100)

The relative equity price of the airline, airport, hotel, and leisure facility sectors has generally fallen since September 11, while prices for insurance brokers have improved.

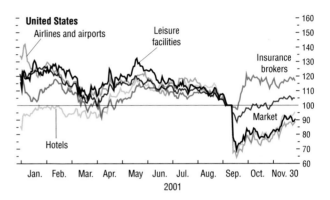

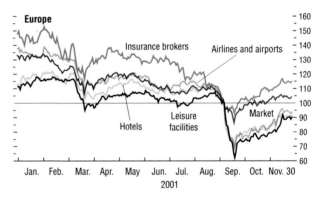

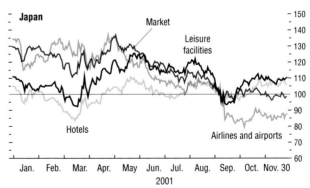

Source: Thomson Financial Datastream.

Box 2.1. The Long-Term Impact of September 11

The main channel through which the continual threat of terrorism could affect the long-term potential of the global economy is by raising transactions costs, resulting in a reduction in potential output. These costs can be broken down as follows:

- *Higher operating costs.* Businesses may experience higher operating costs, owing to increased spending on security, higher insurance premiums, and longer wait times for activities.
- *Higher levels of inventories.* Businesses may be required to hold larger inventories than previously, owing in part to less reliable air and rail transportation. There is anecdotal evidence from the auto industry that production was interrupted because components were not immediately available from suppliers after the September 11 attacks, owing to delays in shipments crossing the U.S.–Canada border.
- *Higher risk premium.* As a result of the attack, lenders' appetite for risk may decline, leading to higher risk premiums that may be passed on to businesses in terms of higher interest rates and lower equity prices, with an adverse effect on investment, and a smaller capital stock.
- *Shift of resources away from the civilian labor force toward the military.* More resources may be diverted toward the military for use in the containment of terrorism. In addition, research and development (R&D) resources may be shifted away from productive activities toward the development of new devices to thwart terrorism (although such devices may have beneficial spillover effects elsewhere).
- *Shift away from globalization.* The attack may have effects on firms' investment decisions—in particular, whether to invest domestically or abroad, in part because of potential disruption of cross-border flows of goods and assets. Costs for such transactions may rise owing to closer inspection of transactions and higher insurance premiums. However, if a new impetus is given to negotiations for a new trade round, other trade barriers could be reduced.

The debate on the impact of the September 11 terrorist attacks on productive potential focuses on two issues on which, given the existing levels of knowledge, people hold widely differing opinions. The first is the extent that "transaction" costs will rise, an issue that depends heavily upon whether further attacks occur, forcing constant high levels of vigilance, or whether September 11 turns out to be a relatively isolated incident, implying a smaller long-term change in behavior. The second is the degree to which a rise in transaction costs will disrupt economic activity, with many arguing that the impact will be limited as firms adapt to new conditions by relatively simple changes in procedures—for example, using more facsimiles and fewer letters if delivery times for the postal service lengthen. Others, however, believe that small transactions costs can lead to significant changes in behavior—for example, the level of trade within countries is much larger than it is between them, presumably reflecting various transactions costs.

Views of the long-term impact divide roughly into three camps:

- *The most commonly held view is that there will be few consequences for the long-term outlook for the United States amd elsewhere.*[1] This assumes that the persistence of the disruptions caused by the terrorist attack will be limited, registering as a small downward shift in productive potential. A useful parallel to assessing the impact may be the assassination of U.S. President John F. Kennedy in 1963. In the days following the murder there was some of the same widespread disbelief that a U.S. President could be assassinated as there has been to the September 11 terrorist attack. Despite the uncertainty following the assassination of President Kennedy, the economy and the equity market strengthened following an initial decline.
- *A significant minority believes that the terrorist attack will have a noticeable impact on productive potential, particularly if additional terrorist activity oc-*

[1]This view was supported by the testimony of Federal Reserve Chairman Alan Greenspan to Congress on October 17, 2001 (Greenspan, 2001).

Box 2.1 *(concluded)*

curs on a sustained basis.[2] This pessimistic view is based on the assumption that the threat of terrorism will create considerable uncertainty, instability, and significantly higher transaction costs. This negative scenario can be compared to the effects of the 1970s oil crises. In both instances there was a shock to the global economy that necessitated a major adjustment in the allocation of resources. In the 1970s, it took several years for productivity to approach its new, somewhat lower, trend.

- *A few argue that the attack will benefit the economy in the long run.* This "creative destruction" view holds that the setback in the economy will enable producers to shed much of their unproductive activities, leading them to adopt newer technologies to become more competitive and thereby enabling the economy to grow at rates in excess of those that prevailed earlier. This positive scenario can be compared to the effects of the Y2K project. In the Y2K case, companies were required to update and improve existing software, which increased their flexibility in adopting new technologies more rapidly.

It is impossible at this stage to provide firm evidence on all of the channels by which the September 11 terrorist attacks could affect long-term potential. That said, rough orders of mag-

nitude can be provided. For example, one private sector analysis estimates the increase to business costs of higher security costs at $1.6 billion per year, the extra financing burden of carrying 10 percent higher inventories at $7.5 billion per year, and an increase in commercial insurance premiums of 20 percent at about $30 billion per year (UBS Warburg, 2001). The total represents about ⅓ percent of nominal GDP. In addition, airlines, hotels, and leisure activity comprise around 2¾ percent of GDP. If the long-term net fall in output in these sectors (i.e., taking into account that spending may rise in other sectors) were a relatively large 10 percent, the loss would be another ¼ percent of GDP. In addition, simulations using MULTI-MOD, the IMF's macroeconomic model, indicate that a half percentage point increase in the costs of capital could reduce the capital stock by 0.2 percent and output by 0.1 percent after five years. The loss in output from all of these sources could be as much as ¾ percent of GDP. Other costs are more difficult to quantify.

To put these costs in perspective, consider the case where long-term potential output in the United States was lowered by 1 percent (about $100 billion)—a relatively generous estimate in the light of the calculations above—while the growth rate of potential remains unchanged. The impact on the five-year average growth rate would be about 0.2 percent, considerably smaller than most estimates of the much-debated impact of information technology on growth since 1996. In short, the impact on potential output would have to be extremely large to be clearly visible when compared to the natural variation in these statistics caused by cyclical phenomena.

[2]For example, a study of the economic effect of conflicts, using the terrorist conflict in the Basque region as a case study, estimates a 10 percentage point decline in real GDP, increasing as terrorist activity rises. See Abadie and Gardeazabal (2001). However, it should be noted that in this case it was relatively easy and cheap to move activities from the Basque region to other places in Spain.

The Confidence Channel

Confidence is a major channel through which the September 11 attacks feed through to the global economy. An unforeseen event of the magnitude of the September 11 terrorist attack can radically alter the view of the future (including the level of uncertainty) for both consumers

and businessmen. This provides an incentive to postpone or cancel spending, which, through Keynesian multiplier and trade channels, can reduce aggregate demand and output at home and in other countries. In addition, data and confidence are available considerably earlier than estimates of activity, and hence can provide

Box 2.2. Financial Market Dislocations and Policy Responses After the September 11 Attacks

The attacks on September 11 damaged some key trading infrastructure and financial intermediaries, resulting in a surge in the demand for liquidity by the U.S. (and to a lesser extent other) financial systems. Concerted policy responses by the United States and other authorities to provide such liquidity were effective in quickly restoring market stability and heading off systemic concerns. In the United States, equities trading was suspended for the week following September 11 and resumed on September 17. Bond trading was suspended September 12 but resumed the next day. Settlements moved from one day to three days that week for Treasury and agency notes, and then were extended to five days for the week starting September 17, but returned to normal thereafter. Early market closure characterized several trading sessions during the crisis period. Policy responses by the U.S. Federal Reserve included, in addition to cuts in interest rates, liquidity injections through the discount window, increases in overnight repos, and augmentations in swap arrangements with other central banks. The injection of liquidity was most evident in the deviation of the federal funds effective rate from its target rate (see the Figure). The U.S. Securities and Exchange Commission also supported the markets' return to normalcy by modifying existing rules on securities lending and share repurchases.

The biggest disruptions to trading infrastructure resulted from damage to the computer and communications systems of the world's largest custodian and settlement bank, the Bank of New York. Manual processing of securities and payment transactions resulted in significantly slower clearing and settlement, generating uncertainty about completion of trades, and demand for liquidity by the financial system. The destruction of the offices of Cantor Fitzgerald, a leading U.S. bond market interdealer broker, and other smaller brokers also led to uncertainty about the settlement of outstanding trades and significant difficulties in brokering new trades.

More broadly, most financial firms located in downtown New York took several days to revert

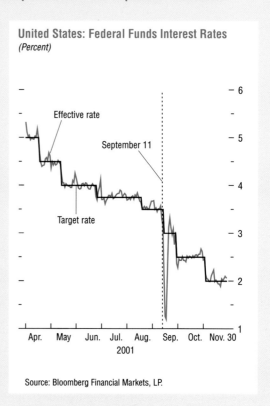

United States: Federal Funds Interest Rates
(Percent)

Effective rate

September 11

Target rate

Apr.   May   Jun.   Jul.   Aug.   Sep.   Oct.   Nov. 30
2001

Source: Bloomberg Financial Markets, LP.

to offsite back-up systems, and perceived or actual delays in transaction settlements reduced the supply of and increased the demand for liquidity in the financial system, even as risk averse investors sought to liquidate positions and increase their cash holdings. While the CHIPS payment system for cross-border foreign exchange transactions was reportedly disrupted for only a few hours on September 11, feared delays in settling the dollar end of cross-border transactions in some instances disrupted overseas trades with a dollar leg. The extraordinary market volatility, and inability to accurately price assets, caused some counterparts to be unable to meet their margin requirements with banks. Recognizing the extraordinary situation, however, banks did not force closing out of these positions, as these were not seen as having the potential of becoming a systemic threat to the financial system.

The U.S. repo market suffered particularly severe dislocations after the September 11 attacks.

Besides being crucial for Treasury bond dealers to finance positions and conduct daily transactions amounting to some $500 billion, the repo market is also the main supplier of short-term liquidity for much of the rest of the financial system, and hence is crucial for orderly financial markets.

Repo transactions were initially affected by damage to trading infrastructure, as well as to firms' absence or lack of full capacity. Consequently, many trades were either "special" (trading near zero percent instead of near the federal funds rate) or "fails" (where both parties were simply unable to complete the trade). As normal trading volumes began to resume and normal settlement rules were re-imposed, fails increased and market participants were increasingly reluctant to lend out securities, further threatening the market. Moreover, many investors actively purchased Treasuries to position their portfolios in safer havens. Weekly fails averaged $45 billion in the second quarter, but reached $400 billion in the week ended September 12, and $1.4 trillion in the week ended September 19. Fails tapered off afterwards, but continued to run at very high levels even after the end of the quarter. The shortage spilled over into the trading of Treasury spot yields, and thereby affected the quoted spreads in markets for swaps and agency and corporate paper. The lack of supply was particularly acute for 5- and 10-year Treasuries. Consequently, the Federal Reserve Bank of New York began pumping an average of $8.5 billion of these securities into the market (while it usually would do less than $1.5 billion), and the Treasury took the unprecedented step of holding an unscheduled auction of $6 billion 10-year Treasury notes on October 5.

useful advanced warning of current cyclical conditions.

While the mechanism through which a reduction in confidence could affect the macroeconomic situation is clear, an assessment of the size of this effect is more complex. Confidence, being a feeling rather than an action, is intrinsically difficult to quantify. In the major industrial countries confidence is measured through surveys that include questions both about the present and next few months, producing a headline figure and separate sub-indices, generally including one that measures future expectations. These surveys differ significantly from country to country in the nature of the questions and the method of compiling the results, but the relative impact of an event can be measured by comparing the change in the index to the "average," defined by the standard deviation of the change in the particular series. The remainder of this section examines how confidence indicators responded to the terrorist attack in comparison to earlier unanticipated events and the predictive value of such confidence indicators for domestic output. In this discussion, the United States is given somewhat more prominence than other countries, reflecting both the location of the terrorist attack, the size of the U.S. economy in the world, and the potential role of an acceleration in U.S. activity in assisting a global recovery.

Figure 2.2 shows the path of U.S. consumer and business confidence since 1985, with the timing of particularly important events marked.[3] As might be expected, confidence is closely linked to the economic cycle, and was declining before September 11. It can also be significantly affected by noneconomic events. The dramatic fall in confidence after the September 11 attacks is clearly one of these events, with consumer and business

[3]Conference Board Surveys are used for both consumer and business confidence. Broadly similar results are seen in other series, in particular the National Association of Purchasing Managers (NAPM) survey of business sentiment and the University of Michigan survey of consumer sentiment, although these surveys indicate some recovery of confidence in November, while the Conference Board data do not.

Figure 2.2. United States: Indicators of Consumer and Business Confidence
(Index numbers)

The fall in consumer and business confidence in the United States after the September 11 attacks is similar to that after Iraq invaded Kuwait.

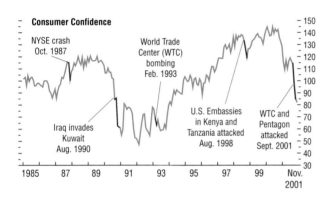

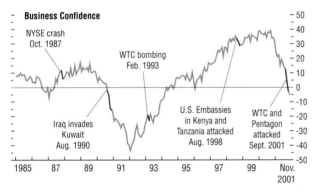

Source: The Conference Board.

confidence between August and October falling by between 2½ and 5 standard deviations—amongst the highest readings—in both cases. These falls are comparable to the impact of the Iraqi invasion of Kuwait (a similarly unpredicted political event that rapidly led to a military response during a period of slowing activity), and considerably larger than other less dramatic terrorist attacks (such as the bombings of the World Trade Center, the U.S. military barracks in Saudi Arabia, U.S. embassies in Africa, or the U.S.S. Cole). Turning to components of the series, the fall in the overall value is somewhat larger (in terms of standard deviations) than the fall in expectations, indicating that the impact may be expected to lessen somewhat over time.

Turning to the rest of the world, business confidence through much of Europe appears to have been hit hard both by the deteriorating economic situation and by the aftermath of the attacks (business confidence in France, Germany, Italy, and, to a somewhat lesser extent, the United Kingdom fell rapidly between August and October, with declines of between ½ and 4 standard deviations), and the forward-looking elements do not appear to have been performing consistently better than assessment of current conditions. The size of the negative impact on consumer sentiment in Europe is generally smaller and more mixed, although, as discussed below, these series generally also have low predictive power. Finally, the September *Tankan* quarterly business survey in Japan and a similar quarterly survey in Canada, whose responses spanned the September 11 tragedy, also plummeted.

The synchronicity of the drops in confidence measures across the major industrial countries, particularly business confidence, probably reflects a range of factors. Underlying business conditions were deteriorating even before the September 11 attacks, especially in Europe and Japan. In addition, changes in business confidence in the United States are often associated with a fall in business confidence elsewhere, presumably reflecting the systemic importance of the United States for other countries (see Box 2.1 of the October 2001 *World Economic Outlook*).

Finally, although the attack was on the United States, the terrorist network appears to have existed in many countries, and hence can be construed as a common shock.

There are several analyses of the impact of consumer confidence on spending in the United States and United Kingdom, most of which conclude it has some impact, but much less work has been done on continental Europe or business confidence.[4] To quantify these effects, the staff undertook an analysis of consumer and business sentiment indices using real GDP for Canada, France, Italy, Japan, the United Kingdom, and the United States since 1985 and Germany since unification.[5] The analysis looked at four issues:

- *Which confidence series are most useful for charting the likely path of the real economy?* The headline figures appear to be the most robust, and are generally a better predictor of trends in output since 1985 than the expectations components (even for future periods) or specific subindices often pointed to as providing superior information.
- *Are changes in confidence rapidly reversed?* When adjusted for the cycle, the lagged change in consumer and business sentiment is rarely important for current levels of confidence, implying that there is no historical reason to expect confidence to improve until recovery starts. However, confidence is likely to be affected by the outcome of noneconomic events, just as U.S. confidence improved after the victory in the Gulf War. In addition, such regressions can be used to examine how much of the recent changes in confidence are a surprise given the cycle. To date, the relevant data are only available for the United States, and indicate that little of the recent falls in confidence are cyclical.
- *How much information do confidence indicators on their own provide about current and future*

output? In the United States, both the business and consumer confidence indicators appear to provide useful information about growth both in the current quarter and the following few quarters. Elsewhere, the business confidence series also provide useful information about the path of growth, but the consumer confidence numbers are less useful (except in Canada). The results imply that, if the fall in confidence since the September attacks in the United States is sustained, output could fall by a percentage point or so, with effects of the order of half of this size elsewhere (Table 2.2).

- *How much additional information do confidence indicators add to simple models of growth?* When other factors that might affect growth in the current period—growth last period, changes in stock prices, and movements in real interest rates—are taken into account, the short-term impact of confidence on growth is generally diminished. However, business confidence in general and consumer confidence in the United States remain useful predictors of movements in real GDP in the future.

In summary, a fall in confidence is a potentially important factor in reducing activity in industrial countries. In the baseline projections, it is assumed that confidence gradually recovers through 2002, so only a portion of the long-run effects on activity are incorporated. More pessimistic assumptions are discussed as part of the alternative scenarios, reported in the appendix to Chapter III.

Financial Market Reaction

Financial markets provide valuable information about how investors perceive the future that both reflects and affects the global outlook. In what follows, it is useful to make a distinction be-

---

[4]On consumer confidence see Acemoglu and Scott (1994); Carroll, Fuhrer, and Wilcox (1994); Bram and Ludvigson (1998); and Macroeconomic Advisors (2001).

[5]More specifically, the change in real GDP was related to current and past changes in confidence, and the coefficients used to calculate the response of output to a downward movement in confidence.

Table 2.2. Impact of Confidence Indices on the Growth of Real GDP
(Percent of GDP, unless otherwise indicated)

	Current Quarter	One Quarter Lag	Two Quarter Lag	Cumulative Impact	Fall in Confidence August to October (Standard Deviations)	Impact on Real GDP If Fall in Confidence Is Sustained
	Impact of a one standard deviation fall in the monthly change in business confidence on real GDP					
United States						
Conference Board	−0.18***	−0.08*	−0.07*	−0.31	3.2	−1.0
NAPM	−0.10**	−0.04	−0.09**	−0.23	4.2	−1.0
Japan	−0.14*[1]	−0.07[1]	−0.06[1]	−0.27[1]	n.a.[2]	n.a.[2]
Germany	−0.10***	−0.05	−0.05	−0.20	3.7	−0.7
France	−0.12***	−0.02	−0.01	−0.15	1.9	−0.3
Italy	−0.11**	−0.09*	−0.02	−0.22	3.0	−0.7
United Kingdom	−0.11**	−0.08*	−0.04*	−0.23	0.5	−0.1
Canada	−0.05[1]	−0.11*[1]	−0.06[1]	−0.22[1]	n.a[2]	n.a.[2]
	Impact of a one standard deviation fall in the monthly change in consumer confidence on real GDP					
United States						
Conference Board	−0.14***	−0.08*	−0.15***	−0.37	5.0	−1.9
University of Michigan	−0.09*	−0.09*	−0.09**	−0.27	2.8	−0.8

Notes: Three asterisks indicate the results are significant at the 1 percent level, two asterisks at the 5 percent level, and one asterisk at the 10 percent level. The coefficients were calculated in such a way that they would be cumulated over time.
[1]As the Japanese and Canadian business confidence data are only available on a quarterly basis, the standard deviations were adjusted down by one-third to reflect the fact that standard deviations of quarterly data tend to be larger than those of monthly data.
[2]Data only available on a quarterly basis.

tween a change in the price of more risky assets caused by an increase in investor risk aversion and a generalized increase in perceived risk. At this time, investor risk aversion, although lower than in the immediate aftermath of September 11, remains evident for high-risk borrowers, most notably emerging market economies but also high-risk borrowers in mature markets. By contrast, broader effects are no longer evident, after a marked rebound in global equity markets.

The terrorist attacks occurred against a backdrop of increasing concerns about global economic activity and corporate earnings, weakening equity markets, and widening high yield and emerging market spreads. They increased what was already an unusually high degree of uncertainty about the near-term outlook and amplified downside risks. Given this backdrop, the global financial market infrastructure showed significant resilience in the immediate aftermath of the attacks despite significant damage to some of the largest U.S. financial institutions and high levels of uncertainty and market volatility.

The main financial market response was a flight to quality that increased borrowing costs for riskier borrowers (Table 2.3). Given the clo-

sure of U.S. equity markets, the immediate market reaction was seen in the credit and currency markets, and in equity markets outside the United States. As in other recent financial crises, including the 1987 stock market crash, the global currency crises in 1997, and the Russian default and LTCM crisis, investors' demand for low-risk assets and cash increased sharply—generally attributed to falling investor risk appetite (see Box 2.3). However, the main beneficiary in this case was cash, seen in the sharp steepening of the U.S. yield curve (which also reflects monetary easing), while U.S. government paper served as less of a safe haven than in past crises as the attacks were on the United States.

The flight to quality affected borrowing costs of high-risk borrowers (Figure 2.3). Spreads on high-yield bonds widened sharply and, compared to high-grade corporates, have remained high. In addition, many smaller companies have been unable to access credit, and the EMBI+ spread on emerging market bonds rose by some 2 percentage points. Initially, the correlation of spreads across emerging market economies rose, indicating a broad based sell-off. More recently, however, these correlations have fallen again, appar-

Table 2.3. Developments in Financial Markets
(Changes in percent, or basis points)

	July 1 Sep. 10	Sep. 11 Sep. 21	Sep. 22 Nov. 27
Equity market (percent)			
S&P 500	−11.7	−11.6	19.0
NASDAQ	−21.1	−16.1	36.0
TOPIX	−17.9	−5.5	8.2
Euro STOXX	−18.2	−17.3	27.6
FTSE 100	−11.9	−11.9	18.8
MSCI Asia	−7.8	−14.4	26.8
MSCI Latin America	−15.4	−13.8	17.5
Credit market (basis points)			
Fed funds target	−25	−50	−100
LIBOR o/n	−56	−120	−25
T-bill, 3-month	−38	−102	−37
Prime lending	−25	−50	−100
T-bond, 10-year	−51	−12	−23
Moody's AAA spread	5	23	−53
Moody's BAA spread	6	24	−52
Merrill Lynch's high yield spread	−21	104	−149
Bloomberg junk bond spread	62	95	−26
EURIBOR, 3-month	−19	−55	−31
EURO bond, 10-year	−24	0	−15
Currency markets (percent)			
Yen/US$	−2.5	−3.7	6.3
US$/Euro	5.9	1.9	−3.4
SF/US$	−5.9	−6.5	4.9
US$/BP	2.8	0.0	−2.9

Sources: Bloomberg; and Datastream.

ently reflecting increasing investor discrimination, while, with the important exception of Argentina, spreads have started to narrow. In short, there appears to have been less of a broad-based financial contagion across industrial and emerging markets and across asset classes than in earlier crises, reflecting the relatively healthier position of financial intermediaries and timely provision of liquidity by central banks.

That said, financing flows to emerging markets in the primary markets have remained weak amidst restricted access to global financial markets. In the emerging markets segment of international bond markets, which has been the most important source for capital account financing for these countries, there had been a sharp reduction in bond issuance beginning in mid-August, although recent data indicate some revival. International equity placements, which had also slowed to a trickle earlier this year, show no indications of recovering, while net syndicated loan flows remain almost flat.

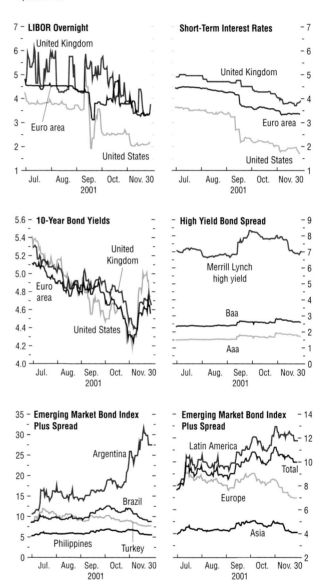

Figure 2.3. Credit and Bond Markets
(In percentage points)

There has been a generalized flight to quality in financial markets since September 11.

Source: Bloomberg Financial Markets, LP.

Box 2.3. Investor Risk Appetite

There is increasing evidence that developments in financial markets are affected as much by changes in risk as in investors' appetite for or aversion to risk (Shiller, 1998). When investors' appetite for risk falls, they reduce their exposure to risky assets, which consequently fall in value together. When investors' appetite for risk rises, risky assets are in increased demand and rise in value together. A fall in risk appetite can also lead to contagion via the portfolios of international investors. A crisis in one country can lead investors to reduce their appetite for risk, which in turn leads them to reduce their exposure to other risky assets as they re-balance their portfolios in terms of risk or liquidity requirements. This phenomenon, labelled the "common creditor," has found some support especially in the Asian and Russian crises (Calvo, 1999; and Allen and Gale, 1999).

A variety of indicators can be used to assess risk appetite. However, most of them appear to proxy for the level of risk, so changes do not necessarily reflect risk appetite. For instance, one commonly used measure is the yield spread between AAA corporate bonds and BBB or lower rated bonds. But this spread may simply reflect the level of risk rather than indicate risk appetite. For instance, the sharp increase in telecom credit spreads since late 1999, given the size of this sector, impacted credit spreads more generally. This could have reflected a combination of an increase in industry specific risk only, an increase in default risk in general, or a decrease in risk appetite. Measures of risk appetite that are based on spreads may therefore also be capturing a combination of changes in risk as well as in risk appetite.[1]

In order to compute a measure of risk appetite, it is important to separate shifts in risk from shifts in risk appetite. One possible procedure is based on the premise that if investors like risk, they will buy assets that have been risky in the past; if they are risk averse, they will sell them. In other words, *if there is a shift in risk ap-*

petite, then we would expect to see the prices of all assets move in proportion to past riskiness. However, *if the level of risk changes,* then movements in prices should not be related to past riskiness. Rather, asset prices will move in tandem with current and expected risk.

To compute a measure based on this procedure, the rank correlation of excess returns and past riskiness for the currencies of the major industrial and emerging market economies are calculated (although other assets would do). The excess returns are computed by examining the returns from holding a currency over a given period relative to expectations, as incorporated in the currency's forward exchange rate; the riskiness of the currencies is proxied by the volatility of excess returns over the preceding 12 months. If the rank correlation is high, changes in excess returns are likely to be due to risk appetite; if low, they would more likely reflect a change in risk (see Persaud, 2001; and Kumar and Persaud, 2001). Such a measure was empirically estimated using daily data for monthly returns and underlying risk for the past decade for 17 currencies. These risk returns correlations provided an index with a value ranging between −1 and +1, with a value closer to −1 indicating low risk appetite, and a value closer to +1 indicating high risk appetite.

The figure shows the daily path of the index measure for the past three months. It indicates that investor risk appetite, which had been weakening prior to the September 11 events, plummeted immediately afterwards. The earlier weakening coincided with increasing concerns about the timing of the recovery in the world economy, and a slew of downgrades for corporate earnings, which would also of course have led to increased risk. Investor risk appetite began to pick up, however, toward the end of September, reflecting in part the prompt policy response, and coincided with the beginning of the rebound in global equity markets. The index then plateaued in mid- to late October, and began to fall in early November (although it has remained positive), possibly reflecting renewed uncertainties about the global economy. The fig-

---

[1]See, for instance, the global risk aversion index regularly published by J.P. Morgan. See also IMF (2001).

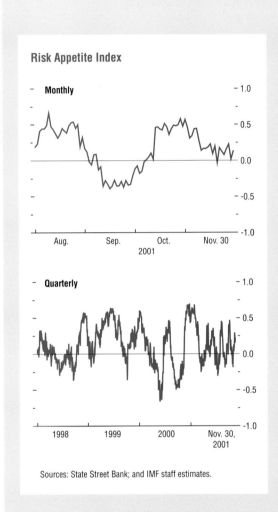

Risk Appetite Index

Monthly

Aug.　Sep.　Oct.　Nov. 30
2001

Quarterly

1998　1999　2000　Nov. 30,
2001

Sources: State Street Bank; and IMF staff estimates.

appetite measure generally precedes an increase in emerging market spreads. Late last year, however, there was some difference in the relative magnitude of the movement in these two, with the risk appetite index rising more than the fall in spreads would imply, indicating a rise in risk. In the immediate aftermath of September 11, a sharp fall in risk appetite and a rise in emerging market risk led to a sharp increase in spreads. More recently, with risk appetite improving but perceived risks for emerging market remaining high, spreads have begun to ease. Similarly, there is a close relationship between changes in this index and changes in corporate credit spreads in the United States, with some evidence that often the appetite measure leads the change in spreads. Over the past month or so, both the increase in risk appetite and some stability in investors' perception of risk in this sector have led to a fall in these credit spreads. More broadly, econometric analysis also shows that the risk appetite index also has a significant power in explaining global financial crises, defined as contemporaneous currency crises in two or more countries, over the past decade.

From a policy perspective, it is useful to distinguish between market sell-offs and financial crisis arising primarily from bad fundamentals and those arising from abrupt shifts in investors' preferences. If crises are due to a falling risk appetite, contagion effects arising from them should be treated differently from those arising from the weakness in fundamentals. In circumstances where a crisis occurs in the wake of declining risk appetite, the financial markets will have a high propensity to react adversely to events that might not otherwise warrant major reaction. In these instances, responding quickly to a crisis could substantially reduce its magnitude and potential spillovers.

ure also shows the evolution of a less volatile version of the index over the past three years. The index hit lows on four occasions corresponding to the Russian–LTCM crisis, ahead of the Y2K concerns, around the collapse of the tech bubble in April 2000, and in the third quarter of last year when uncertainties about rising oil prices and possible global stagflation began to mount.

A comparison of the evolution of the index and EMBI+ spread shows that a fall in the risk

In the major currency markets, the currencies of capital exporting countries like Japan and Switzerland initially strengthened as the home bias in investors' decisions appeared to be more

pronounced compared to earlier episodes. Subsequently, the major currencies stabilized relatively quickly, reflecting in part the synchronized global business cycle under way as well as

Box 2.4. How Did the September 11 Attacks Affect Exchange Rate Expectations?

The immediate impact of the September 11 attacks in the United States on major exchange rates was moderate and dissipated within a month of the attacks. In the first week after the attacks, the dollar depreciated 3 to 4 percent against the yen and the euro, exacerbating the decline that began in July. However, amid growing confidence that relative performance during a global slowdown would favor the United States, in part due to policy stimulus, the dollar has rebounded since mid-September to levels above those prevailing just prior to the attack.

Information extracted from currency option prices can be used to infer market expectations about the likelihood that different values of future exchange rates will occur.[1] These probabilities can be interpreted as the market's view of the (risk-neutral) likelihood of different exchange rate values at a given future date (three months in the analysis below) around the forward rate.[2]

There are several main conclusions that can be drawn from comparing market expectations at several points in time since the attacks (see the figure). The decline of the dollar in the spot market in the week following the attacks prompted currency derivatives traders to center their dollar expectations on more pessimistic levels. For example, whereas on September 10 the market attached virtually no weight to the euro-dollar rate reaching parity three months out, a week later the market was placing considerable weight on that possibility. Spreading uncertainty and the rising potential for large changes in the weeks after the attack initially resulted in a wider dispersion of beliefs about future yen and euro values, and thus a larger variance of extracted probability distributions. By October, amid receding exchange rate uncertainty, on average dealers priced in a slight dollar appreciation with a higher precision compared to pre-attack levels.

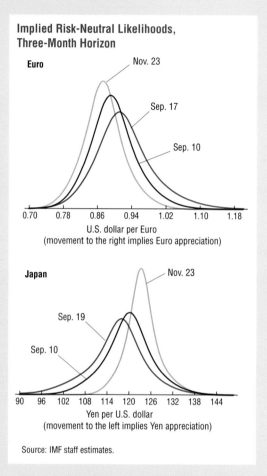

Implied Risk-Neutral Likelihoods, Three-Month Horizon

Euro

Nov. 23
Sep. 17
Sep. 10

0.70   0.78   0.86   0.94   1.02   1.10   1.18
U.S. dollar per Euro
(movement to the right implies Euro appreciation)

Japan

Nov. 23
Sep. 19
Sep. 10

90   96   102   108   114   120   126   132   138   144
Yen per U.S. dollar
(movement to the left implies Yen appreciation)

Source: IMF staff estimates.

The attacks heightened previously existing expectations among currency option traders that the likelihood of a sharp dollar depreciation was greater than that of an equally sharp appreciation over the following three months. While the forward premium offered little information on market sentiment that was not also embedded in the spot exchange rate, expectations extracted from currency options had been skewed toward a declining dollar against the yen and the euro since July 2001. For example, the price of options that insure against an appreciation relative to the price of options that insure against a depreciation (the so-called risk reversal price) had already implied a dollar depreciation since August. In the wake of the attacks, risk reversal prices reached a 10-month peak in the yen-dollar market and a 36-month

---

[1]This box uses the smoothed method proposed by Malz (1997).

[2]Risk-neutral probabilities combine the "true" expected probability with the market's equilibrium attitude toward risk.

peak in the euro-dollar market. The sudden decline of these prices in October as the dollar recaptured its safe haven role reflects the markedly lower risk of a dollar depreciation that has been priced in currency option markets since that time. Thus, the effect of the at-

tack on exchange rate expectations was considerable but very short-lived and was reversed within one month, as traders quickly regained confidence in the dollar amid higher political uncertainty and indications of increasing synchronicity in business cycles.

the safe haven effect (see Box 2.4). However, increased risk aversion had a negative impact on emerging markets, and those with high external financing requirements in particular saw their currencies come under sustained pressure as access to international capital markets was expected to be severely curtailed. The currencies of commodity exporting countries also weakened sharply on the expectation that slower world growth would further weaken commodity prices.

In global equity markets, there was a sharp increase in price volatility and transactions volumes, as expectations of future risks and returns went through a major reappraisal, amidst heightened uncertainty about fundamentals. All major stock markets experienced rapid, sharp price declines, reflecting expectations about the adverse impact of the tragedy on corporate profitability and portfolio reshuffling, as investors' demand for liquid, less risky assets increased. The emerging equity markets followed the industrial country markets, with a clear increase in cross-country correlation between industrial and emerging market economies, and among emerging market economies. However, equity price indices began to rise again on September 24 in all major and emerging country stock markets, and by October 11, broad stock price indices in mature markets were back at the levels registered prior to September 11, generally continuing to rise thereafter (see Chapter I, Figure 1.2). In emerging markets, however, the recovery has generally been less vigorous.

This rebound is faster than in earlier episodes of crisis, such as Iraq's invasion of Kuwait in mid-1998 or the LTCM crisis in late 1998, and may appear surprising given the generalized increase in uncertainty and weakening global prospects. However, the rebound could be explained by the benefits to profits from the vigorous policy response or by the impact of lower short-term interest rates on the speed with which future expected rates are discounted. In view of these changes in fundamentals, a key question is, given the decline in nominal interest rates, what changes in earnings growth are consistent with roughly unchanged or slightly higher stock prices? Illustrative scenarios based on a standard present-value approach widely used in the valuation of equities can be used to gauge changes in investors' earnings expectations after September 11 in four major stock markets.[6] The September 11 event is treated as a shock, which temporarily affects nominal interest rates and earnings growth for a period of one year. After that, future earnings growth is assumed to return to the medium-term values considered sustainable by investors on September 10.

Results were calculated for three dates, September 21 (when broad price indices for all major stock markets reached their low), October 11 (when price indices surpassed their September 10 levels), and November 26 (Table 2.4). The calculations take the change in the price-earnings ratio and short and long-term interest rates to estimate the implied change in expected earnings on the next year. For the United States, although

---

[6]In the model, future dividend growth is assumed proportional to future earning growth (see Campbell, Lo, and Mackinlay, 1997).

Table 2.4. Change in the Implied Earnings Growth Rates over the Next Year[1]

(Percent over the next year)

	Deviations from September 10 values		
	Sept. 21	Oct. 11	Nov. 26
United States			
S&P 500	−11.1	−5.2	−0.6
Datastream index	−11.7	0.3	13.1
Japan			
Topix	−7.0	−1.6	0.8
Datastream index	−5.3	0.8	7.0
Germany			
DAX	−18.0	4.8	25.6
Datastream index	−21.3	0.0	14.8
United Kingdom			
Financial Times SE100	−11.9	1.2	6.7
Datastream index	−11.2	3.3	9.2

Sources: Datastream; and IMF staff calculations.
[1]See text for calculation of implied earnings growth rates.

the precise results are sensitive to the index used in the calculations, they demonstrate how investors expected a substantial temporary decline in earnings growth immediately after the attacks. However, investor pessimism did not last long, and by November 26 investors had priced in only a small temporary decline in the average earnings growth rate during the next four quarters (the broader DataStream index indicates investors were significantly more positive). In Japan, markets have also priced in either no change or an increase in earnings growth, and in Germany and the United Kingdom expected earnings growth for the next four quarters is now substantially above the September 10 baseline. This suggests that the aggressive monetary easing

after September 11 may not be the only reason for the rebound in stock prices, and investors expect the adverse effects of the September 11 attack to be largely confined to the United States.

Buoyant market expectations appear to have been a stabilizing factor in stock market developments after an initial period of turbulence. However, this optimism could also increase the vulnerability of equity markets to disappointment, both with regard to the timing of the recovery and the medium-term outlook. In particular, the consensus forecast for pre-tax profits in the United States and elsewhere has been revised downward significantly for this year and the next, and continues to be highly uncertain (Table 2.5). This is in marked contrast with the widespread expectations by equity analysts of a rapid recovery, as reflected in the double-digit earnings growth rate projected in 2002 for the U.S. S&P 500 index by analysts. Regarding the medium-term earnings outlook, equity analysts forecast an average five-year growth in earnings per share for the S&P 500 index of about 12.5 percent, roughly 4 percent above the average rate during 1996–2000. There appear to be downside risks to this outlook given the persistence of a weaker business environment in the major advanced economies, with continuing excess capacity, intense competition, and further declines in corporate profit margins.

Commodity Markets

Commodity markets provide a way of cushioning the impact of the fall in activity in industrial

Table 2.5. United States: Consensus Forecasts During January–October 2001 for Pre-Tax Profits[1]

(Annual change in percent)

Forecast of	Jan.	Feb.	March	April	May	June	July	Aug.	Sept.[2]	Oct.	Nov.
2001 average	2.2	0.0	−1.9	−3.8	−3.4	−4.6	−8.6	−10.7	−11.7	−15.9	−15.5
(Standard deviation)	3.1	3.6	4.2	3.4	3.7	2.6	1.7	4.8	2.1	2.5	2.8
2002 average	6.6	5.8	5.9	5.2	5.6	4.8	5.8	4.6	3.9	2.1	0.4
(Standard deviation)	3.7	4.2	2.6	3.2	3.1	3.0	3.4	5.2	3.8	6.6	8.0

Source: Consensus Forecast.
[1]Average and standard deviation of monthly forecasts for annual earnings growth in 2001 and 2002 by 19 participants in the survey conducted by Consensus Forecast.
[2]Survey conducted before September 11, 2001.

countries, but at the cost of worse prospects for many developing countries dependent on such exports. Prices of primary commodities, which were already weakening in the face of lower world growth, fell further in the wake of the September 11 terrorist attacks. World oil prices declined to around $18 per barrel by late November from over $25 prior to the attacks and the peak of over $30 reached in 2000, and the baseline path is around 25 percent below that in the October 2001 *World Economic Outlook* for 2002. For nonfuel commodities, a weaker demand outlook has reinforced the effects of secular increases in supply for some key commodities.

Recent Developments

After fluctuating around $20 per barrel through early November, oil prices softened further in response to OPEC's difficulties in coordinating global production cuts, particularly among non-OPEC producers. Most significantly, Russian commitments fell short of the 200,000 barrels per day cut envisaged by OPEC. While discussions among producers continued, the futures price for 2002 delivery fell to $18 per barrel in late November and futures markets project relatively weak prices through 2002. The near-term outlook for prices clearly depends on the willingness of exporters to agree on production limits. Even if agreement is reached, however, the scope for significant price increases is limited by weak global demand and incentives for producers to circumvent agreed limits if prices rise.

Prices of most nonfuel commodities have also fallen since the terrorist attacks. The IMF's aggregate index of nonfuel prices dropped by a further 6 percent from September to November 2001, bringing the overall decline since the beginning of 2000 to 14 percent, largely reflecting weaker world demand. For several agricultural commodities, notably coffee and cotton, this has reinforced existing imbalances arising from expanding supply. Coffee prices have dropped to less than half their end-1999 levels, as producers such as Brazil and Vietnam have continued to raise production by more than the normal ex-

pansion of world consumption. For cotton, prices have fallen by about 30 percent over the past two years, and are at one-third of their 1995 peaks. Technological changes have boosted supply and competition has increased from synthetic fibers, while U.S. agriculture subsidies have made U.S. cotton prices highly competitive, resulting in a sharp increase in U.S. cotton exports that have further depressed world prices. The slump in metals prices has been compounded since September 11. Copper, aluminum, tin, and nickel prices have dropped by between 25 and 50 percent since the end of 1999, as inventories have accumulated. Timber prices surged in 1999 and early 2000 as the U.S. housing market boomed, but subsequently fell back as demand prospects deteriorated; market conditions remain vulnerable to the outcome of a trade dispute on lumber products between the United States and Canada.

Global semiconductor prices, production, and sales weakened through the third quarter, led by the collapse in the market for memory chips. The dollar value of DRAM shipments in the third quarter was only 20 percent of the same period of 2000, reflecting sharply lower prices and volumes, while shipments of other semiconductors fell by about one-half over the same period. Sales of final products, particularly computers, have remained sluggish in recent months, although DRAM prices have stabilized somewhat lately and inventories are falling, indicating the downturn may be ending. However, two key ratios—capital investment to revenues and new orders to recently completed orders—indicate the bottom of the cycle has probably not been reached and will occur sometime during 2002. For 2002 as a whole, industry analysts are forecasting a modest increase in both prices and unit sales that, while an improvement over 2001, would be well below historical norms.

Lower Prices and Commodity Exporters

Declines in commodity prices have lowered overall prices in major countries, increasing real incomes and creating scope for more aggressive monetary easing in response to the global downturn. On the whole, this is beneficial for global growth, as the propensity to consume of oil consumers is higher than that for oil producers.[7] For commodity exporters, however, lower prices cause a deterioration in the terms of trade. This shock is likely to negatively affect real activity in exporters through both direct and indirect linkages. The direct relationship between the price and volume of commodity production is ambiguous, depending on whether lower prices reflect lower demand or higher supply. A demand decrease—of the type experienced in the wake of the September 11 attacks—would reduce output; a supply increase, in contrast, would raise it. These direct relationships between prices and activity are likely to occur fairly contemporaneously. The indirect effects reflect the impact of changes in the terms of trade on real incomes and spending, and are unambiguous. A deterioration in the terms of trade will reduce spending in the producing country on both domestic and imported goods. Domestic output will fall unless some other factor, such as policy settings, adjusts in a way that more than offsets the shock to private demand. These indirect effects are likely to occur with a lag, as domestic spending exhibits inertia in response to changes in income.

To assess the importance of these effects for developing countries, regressions were estimated relating growth in real output in developing country commodity producers to changes in the terms of trade due to commodity price movements. For this purpose, a series was constructed for each exporting country that reflected the effect of commodity price changes on the trade balance, expressed as a percent of GDP. These effects are static, or "first-order," in the sense that they do not incorporate the induced impact on volumes of relative price movements. Real GDP growth for the full panel was then regressed on the current and lagged values of these terms-of-trade effects, and the results are reported in Table 2.6. Shocks to the terms of

Table 2.6. Estimated Effects of Commodity Price Changes on GDP Growth
(t statistics in parentheses)

	Current Value	Lagged Value
Nonfuel exporters	0.009 (0.18)	0.196 (4.19)
Fuel exporters	0.086 (2.04)	0.104 (2.11)

Note: Panel regression of change in the logarithm of real GDP on a country-specific constant term and the current and lagged values of the impact of commodity price movements on the terms of trade expressed as a percent of GDP. Kuwait was excluded from the group of fuel exporters due to data volatility associated with the Gulf War.

trade have little contemporaneous impact on activity for the nonfuel exporters. This is consistent with the ambiguous nature of the direct effects of price changes, the fact that prices for farmers are often fixed in the short-term (and many major producers also take out long-term, fixed-price contracts), and that crop rotations are different from calendar years. With a lag of one year, the coefficient is significantly positive: an improvement in the trade balance of 1 percent of GDP arising from commodity price movements is associated with an increase in real output growth of 0.2 percentage points. For fuel exporters, the aggregate impact is roughly the same, but the effects are distributed more evenly between the current and lagged values, suggesting that the indirect effects may work faster in these countries.

These results imply that recent commodity price movements will have their greatest effect on fuel exporters, reflecting the large fall in oil prices. The projected decline in world oil prices of 35 percent from 2000 to 2002 implies a decline in the terms of trade of this group of about 10 percent of GDP and a decline of real GDP of 2 percent or more (given it is a demand side shock), although this may well overestimate the impact as the more conservative policies followed by many oil exporters over the latest cycle—when more of the oil windfall revenues were saved than in previous episodes—will re-

[7]However, to the extent that lower prices reduce the incentive to invest in production facilities, they can reduce supply capacity, thereby increasing the likelihood of a price spike when activity accelerates, as occurred in 2000.

duce the amplitude of the boom-bust cycle. For nonfuel exporters, the effects are smaller, as declines in prices of imports of manufactured goods and oil have moderated the effect of lower export prices—a similar calculation points to a drop of less than ¼ percent in GDP due to terms of trade movements.

That being said, for many poor nonfuel commodity exporting countries the growth numbers may understate the impact on poverty. Lower prices for agricultural goods will hurt rural areas, where most of the poor live, while the benefits of lower oil prices tend to accrue in urban areas, and within these urban areas often to the middle class who have the means to buy oil-based fuels for heat rather than using wood.

References

Abadie, Alberto, and Javier Gardeazabal, 2001, "The Economic Costs of Conflict: A Case-Control Study for the Basque Country," NBER Working Paper No. 8478 (Cambridge, Mass.: National Bureau of Economic Research).

Acemoglu, Daron, and Andrew Scott, 1994, "Consumer Confidence and Rational Expectations: Are Agents' Beliefs Consistent with Theory," *Economic Journal,* Vol. 104 (January), pp. 1–20.

Allen, Franklin, and Douglas Gale, 1999, "Financial Contagion," Starr Center for Applied Economics, Economic Research Reports No. 98–33, New York University.

Bram, Jason, and Sydney Ludvigson, 1998, "Does Consumer Confidence Forecast Household Expenditure? A Sentiment Index Horse Race," *Economic Policy Review,* Federal Reserve Bank of New York (June), pp. 59–78.

Calvo, Guillermo, 1999, "Contagion in Emerging Markets," (unpublished; Department of Economics, University of Maryland).

Campbell, John, 1999, "Asset Prices, Consumption and the Business Cycle," in *The Handbook of Macro-economics,* ed. by John B. Taylor and Michael Woodford (Amsterdam; New York: North-Holland).

Campbell, John Y., and Andrew Lo, and Craig MacKinlay, 1997, *The Econometrics of Financial Markets* (Princeton: Princeton University Press).

Carroll, Christopher, Jeffrey Fuhrer, and David Wilcox, 1994, "Does Consumer Sentiment Forecast Consumer Spending? If So, Why?" *American Economic Review,* Vol. 81 (December), pp. 1397–1408.

Greenspan, Allen, 2001, statement before the Joint Economic Committee of the U.S. Congress, October 17. Available on the Internet at *www.federalreserve.gov.*

IMF, 2001, *Emerging Markets Financing,* International Monetary Fund, third quarter (November). Available on the Internet at *www.imf.org/external/pubs/ft/emf/index.htm.*

Kumar, Manmohan, and Avinash Persaud, 2001, "Pure Contagion and Investors' Shifting Risk Appetite: Analytical Issues and Empirical Evidence," IMF Working Paper No. 01/134 (Washington: International Monetary Fund).

Macroeconomic Advisors, 2001, *Economic Outlook,* October 15, Vol. 19:9.

Malz, Allan, 1997, "Estimating the Probability Distribution of the Future Exchange Rate from Option Prices," *The Journal of Derivatives,* (Winter), pp. 18–35.

Persaud, Avinash, 2001, "Fads and Fashions in the Policy Response to Financial Market Crises," in *Financial Innovations and the Welfare of Nations,* ed. by L. Jacque and P.M. Vaaler (Boston: Kluwer Academic Publishers).

Shiller, Robert, 1998, "Human Behavior and the Efficiency of the Financial System," NBER Working Paper No. 6375 (Cambridge, Mass.: National Bureau of Economic Research).

UBS Warburg, 2001, *Global Economic Strategy Research,* October 12.

U.S. Bureau of Economic Analysis, 2001a, *Survey of Current Business,* November.

———, 2001b, "Gross Domestic Product: Third quarter 2001 (Preliminary). Corporate Profits: Third quarter 2001 (Preliminary)," News Release, November 30.

CHAPTER III

GLOBAL AND REGIONAL ECONOMIC PROSPECTS

The tragic events of September 11 came at a time when, with all major regions already slowing, the global economy was particularly vulnerable to adverse shocks. Indeed, recent data suggest that the world economy was weaker than earlier thought even before the terrorist attacks. Furthermore, these attacks—while affecting the United States most directly—can clearly be seen as a shock with global reach, given the worldwide impact on confidence, financial markets, and growth prospects.

The Global Outlook

Reflecting these developments, the IMF's projections for almost all regions of the world have been marked down compared with those in the October 2001 *World Economic Outlook* (whose projections were finalized before the terrorist attacks). These reductions are most apparent in the outlook for 2002, where the strengthening of activity that had previously been expected in late 2001—particularly among advanced economies—is now generally not expected until around the middle of 2002. Growth in the advanced economies is now expected to be only 0.8 percent in 2002, down from a weak 1.1 percent in 2001 (Table 3.1). The outlook for 2002 is 1¼ percentage points lower than projected in the October *World Economic Outlook*, including reductions of about 1½ percentage points in the United States, Japan, and Canada, 1 percentage point in the euro area, and over 2 percentage points in the newly industrialized Asian economies (see Table 1.1 in Chapter I). For developing countries as a whole, the growth projection for 2002 has been lowered by nearly 1 percentage point, with the largest reductions among countries of the Western Hemisphere—especially Argentina and Mexico—and also among the members of the Association of South East Asian Nations (ASEAN). Nevertheless, growth of close to 4½

percent is expected for the developing country group in 2002 compared with 4 percent in 2001, supported by relatively strong activity in China and India, a significant turnaround in Turkey's economic prospects, and reasonably firm growth in the transition economies and Africa.

The limited amount of data since the terrorist attacks against which to gauge economic prospects and the virtually unprecedented nature of these recent events inevitably imply a high level of uncertainty in the latest projections. Particular concerns are the prospective depth and duration of the general downturn in confidence and activity, the risk that existing weaknesses in some sectors (such as information technology) will be exacerbated, the addition of new sectoral pressures (e.g., in travel and tourism), and the vulnerabilities apparent in some systemically important countries. At a more general level, forecasters have not been particularly successful in capturing turning points in the cycle and the ensuing pace of activity, and this needs to be taken into account when policy responses are being considered. Over the past decade, however, the IMF's global growth forecasts have been generally unbiased—although with substantial variation in region-by-region performance—and the mean and standard deviation of the forecast errors for the Group of Seven countries are similar to those of private forecasters (Box 3.1).

United States and Canada

Almost all economic indicators in the United States have weakened in recent months. While part of this downturn reflects greater-than-expected weakness in the economy before September 11, the attacks and their aftermath led to further declines—including among indicators such as consumer spending and nondefense durable goods orders that had signaled a

Table 3.1. Advanced Economies: Real GDP, Consumer Prices, and Unemployment
(Annual percent change and percent of labor force)

	Real GDP				Consumer Prices				Unemployment			
	1999	2000	2001	2002	1999	2000	2001	2002	1999	2000	2001	2002
Advanced economies	**3.3**	**3.9**	**1.1**	**0.8**	**1.4**	**2.3**	**2.3**	**1.3**	**6.4**	**5.8**	**6.0**	**6.6**
Major advanced economies	3.0	3.5	1.0	0.6	1.4	2.3	2.2	1.1	6.1	5.7	6.0	6.6
United States	4.1	4.1	1.0	0.7	2.2	3.4	2.9	1.6	4.2	4.0	4.9	6.0
Japan	0.7	2.2	−0.4	−1.0	−0.3	−0.8	−0.7	−1.0	4.7	4.7	5.0	5.7
Germany	1.8	3.0	0.5	0.7	0.7	2.1	2.4	1.0	8.2	7.5	7.5	7.8
France	3.0	3.5	2.1	1.3	0.6	1.8	1.8	1.1	11.2	9.5	8.6	8.9
Italy	1.6	2.9	1.8	1.2	1.7	2.6	2.6	1.3	11.4	10.6	9.5	9.4
United Kingdom[1]	2.1	2.9	2.3	1.8	2.3	2.1	2.3	2.4	6.0	5.6	5.2	5.4
Canada	5.1	4.4	1.4	0.8	1.7	2.7	2.8	1.6	7.6	6.8	7.3	8.0
Other advanced economies	4.9	5.2	1.5	1.9	1.3	2.4	2.9	1.8	7.3	6.2	6.2	6.3
Spain	4.1	4.1	2.7	2.1	2.2	3.4	3.6	2.1	15.9	14.1	13.0	12.8
Netherlands	3.7	3.5	0.9	1.0	2.0	2.3	5.1	2.1	3.2	2.6	2.4	3.7
Belgium	3.0	4.0	1.2	0.7	1.1	2.7	2.4	0.5	8.8	7.0	6.9	8.1
Sweden	4.1	3.6	1.2	1.7	0.5	1.0	2.6	2.3	5.6	4.7	4.1	4.1
Austria	2.8	3.3	1.1	1.3	0.5	2.0	2.4	2.0	3.9	3.7	3.8	4.1
Denmark	2.1	3.2	1.3	1.7	2.5	3.0	2.4	2.7	5.6	5.2	5.2	5.3
Finland	4.0	5.7	0.7	1.8	1.3	3.0	2.6	1.7	10.3	9.8	9.4	9.9
Greece	3.4	4.3	4.1	3.0	2.2	2.9	3.6	2.9	12.0	11.4	10.9	10.9
Portugal	3.4	3.2	1.6	0.8	2.2	2.8	4.3	2.7	4.4	4.0	3.9	4.2
Ireland	10.9	11.5	6.1	3.0	2.5	5.3	3.9	2.8	5.6	4.3	3.8	4.5
Luxembourg	7.6	8.5	3.3	3.2	1.0	3.2	2.5	2.1	2.9	2.6	2.7	2.7
Switzerland	1.6	2.9	1.6	0.8	0.8	1.6	1.0	0.8	2.7	1.9	1.9	2.4
Norway	1.1	2.3	1.7	2.0	2.3	3.1	3.1	1.9	3.2	3.4	3.4	3.7
Israel	2.6	6.2	0.3	1.7	5.2	1.1	1.2	1.8	8.9	8.8	9.0	9.5
Iceland	4.1	3.6	1.9	0.5	3.4	5.1	6.5	6.7	1.9	1.4	1.4	2.0
Cyprus	4.5	5.1	4.0	3.0	1.8	4.1	2.0	1.8	3.6	3.4	3.6	3.8
Korea	10.9	8.8	2.6	3.2	0.8	2.3	4.3	2.0	6.3	4.1	3.8	3.5
Australia[2]	4.7	3.3	2.3	3.3	1.5	4.5	4.2	2.2	7.0	6.3	6.8	7.0
Taiwan Province of China	5.4	6.0	−2.2	0.7	0.2	1.3	−0.1	0.3	2.9	3.0	5.1	5.0
Hong Kong SAR	3.0	10.5	−0.3	1.0	−4.0	−3.7	−1.5	—	6.3	5.0	5.1	5.9
Singapore	5.9	9.9	−2.9	1.2	0.1	1.4	1.0	1.4	3.5	3.1	4.5	4.2
New Zealand[2]	3.8	3.8	2.6	1.9	1.1	2.7	2.7	2.2	6.8	6.0	5.3	5.5
Memorandum												
European Union	2.6	3.4	1.7	1.3	1.4	2.3	2.7	1.6	9.1	8.1	7.6	7.8
Euro area	2.6	3.4	1.5	1.2	1.1	2.4	2.7	1.4	10.0	8.9	8.3	8.6

[1]Consumer prices are based on the retail price index excluding mortgage interest.
[2]Consumer prices excluding interest rate components; for Australia, also excluding other volatile items.

possible bottoming out of activity prior to the attacks. The initial sharp fall-off in some indicators has at least partially reversed since September—helped in the case of retail sales, for example, by significant sales incentives for automobiles—but most indicators of household and business activity continue to suggest that growth remains subdued in the latter part of 2001 (Figure 3.1). In the labor market, for example, job losses and new claims for unemployment benefits in October reached their highest levels since the early 1990s and, although slowing since then, point to further increases in the unemployment

rate in the months ahead. The housing market appeared surprisingly robust through August, but recently released indicators suggest that a substantial slowing is in prospect. Moreover, some sectors, particularly travel and entertainment, have faced particularly severe financial difficulties since September 11 (see Chapter II).

Nevertheless, various forces should contribute to a strengthening recovery in 2002, although the speed and strength of their impact is difficult to anticipate. These forces include the recent reduction in energy prices, the ending of the inventory cycle downturn, the recovery in

Figure 3.1. Macroeconomic Indicators—Advanced Economies

Most indicators of economic activity and confidence have weakened sharply since 2000.

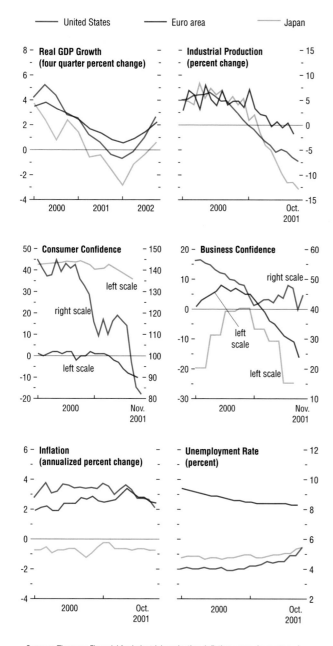

Sources: Thomson Financial for industrial production, inflation, unemployment, and consumer and business confidence for the United States and Japan; European Central Bank for euro area industrial production, inflation, and unemployment; European Commission for euro area consumer and business confidence.

equity prices, and somewhat stronger levels of consumer and business sentiment about the future compared to the present. Most important, there is now significant macroeconomic stimulus in the pipeline. On the monetary side, official interest rates have been reduced by 4¾ percentage points since the beginning of 2001, including 1¾ percentage points since September 11, and there is scope for additional easing if economic conditions weaken further. The easing to date has spurred a record surge in the refinancing of home mortgages, which should help sustain spending in the household sector, and further support to demand can be expected given the lags between interest rate cuts and their impact on activity. Fiscal policy has also been eased substantially during 2001, including in response to the events of September 11; rapid implementation of additional stimulus as currently under discussion—if carefully designed to strengthen consumer confidence and boost activity in the short run—would provide further helpful support for recovery (see Box 3.2). As the economy recovers, however, tax or spending measures may be needed to ensure that medium-term Social Security obligations can be met.

In the baseline projections for the United States, the decline in economic activity is expected to stabilize in early 2002, with a firmer pickup emerging in the second half of the year. Overall, the growth projection for 2002 has been marked down to 0.7 percent, 1½ percentage points lower than in the previous *World Economic Outlook* (whose projections were finalized before the attacks). Given the expected strengthening of activity during the year, however, growth would reach over 2½ percent in the fourth quarter of 2002 compared with the same quarter of 2001. Substantial uncertainty still surrounds this short-term outlook. A stronger and more rapid recovery could emerge if confidence rebounds rapidly, oil prices fall more than anticipated, or the inventory cycle downturn ends quickly. On the other side, concerns about personal security and rising unemployment, together with the sharp downturn in corporate profitability and the difficulties faced by some specific sectors, could

Box 3.1. The Accuracy of *World Economic Outlook* Growth Forecasts: 1991–2000

Each issue of the *World Economic Outlook* includes forecasts of economic growth for the world and for various country groupings. By their nature, forecasts are subject to uncertainty, which—as extensively discussed elsewhere in this issue—needs to be explicitly taken into account by policymakers when considering the implications for policy. This Box reports some indicators of the accuracy of the *World Economic Outlook* growth forecasts over the period 1991 through 2000.[1] It is important to stress, however, that the historical record with respect to the forecast accuracy of the *World Economic Outlook* is not necessarily a good guide to the future. For example, IMF forecasts—like those of outside analysts—tend to underestimate growth during booms and overestimate growth during recessions. Thus, as discussed further below, forecast accuracy depends importantly on the time period in question, and the specific events that occurred during it.

The first table presents the mean and standard deviation of the forecast error, defined as the difference between the growth forecast and the actual outturn, for various country groupings over the period 1991–2000.[2] The average error provides an indication of whether the forecast was subject to bias over the period—a positive value, for example, shows that growth was on average overestimated; the standard deviation of the error provides a measure of the degree of uncertainty in the forecast. The forecast errors are shown at four different points in

[1]The forecasts for the Group of Seven countries are evaluated over the period from 1985 through 2000.

[2]The outturn is taken from the October issue of the *World Economic Outlook* one year after the year in question.

World Economic Outlook: Estimates of GDP Growth Forecast Errors[1]

	Spring of Previous Year		Fall of Previous Year		Spring of Current Year		Fall of Current Year	
	Average error	Standard deviation	Average error	Standard deviation	Average error	Standard deviation	Average error	Standard deviation
World[2]	**0.4**	**0.9**	**0.2**	**0.9**	**−0.1**	**0.5**	**−0.1**	**0.3**
Advanced economies	0.4	1.2	0.2	1.1	−0.1	0.6	—	0.4
Major advanced economies	0.4	1.2	0.2	1.1	—	0.6	0.1	0.4
United States	−0.5	1.7	−0.5	1.5	−0.2	0.9	—	0.7
Japan	1.8	2.1	1.4	1.9	0.3	1.3	0.2	0.4
Germany	0.9	1.5	0.8	1.5	0.1	1.0	0.2	0.8
France	0.8	1.3	0.6	1.5	0.1	0.8	—	0.5
Italy	1.1	1.2	0.8	1.0	0.3	0.8	0.2	0.5
United Kingdom	0.7	1.6	0.5	1.5	−0.2	0.8	−0.2	0.4
Canada	0.9	2.2	0.6	1.8	0.2	1.2	0.1	0.7
Other advanced economies	0.3	1.4	0.1	1.5	−0.2	1.0	−0.2	0.5
Developing countries	0.2	1.4	—	1.1	−0.3	0.7	−0.2	0.4
Africa	1.9	1.2	1.6	1.0	1.2	0.7	0.6	0.5
Sub-Saharan	1.7	1.3	1.5	1.0	1.0	0.7	0.6	0.4
Developing Asia	−0.6	2.2	−0.7	2.0	−0.7	1.3	−0.3	0.7
ASEAN-4[3]	1.7	5.7	1.3	5.2	0.4	3.0	—	0.9
Middle East, Malta, and Cyprus	0.6	2.0	0.9	2.6	0.5	2.6	−0.2	1.3
Western Hemisphere	1.0	1.8	0.7	1.3	−0.4	1.1	−0.3	0.9
Memorandum								
World[4]	0.7	1.2	0.5	1.2	0.1	0.8	—	0.5
Countries in transition	6.0	6.6	4.5	6.3	2.6	6.4	−0.6	1.2

[1]Forecast errors are defined as forecast minus outturn. Sample period covers 1990 to 2000.
[2]Excludes countries in transition.
[3]Includes Indonesia, Malaysia, the Philippines, and Thailand.
[4]Includes countries in transition.

Box 3.1 *(concluded)*

Consensus Forecast: Estimates of GDP Growth Forecast Errors[1]

	Spring of Previous Year		Fall of Previous Year		Spring of Current Year		Fall of Current Year	
	Average errors	Standard deviation	Average errors	Standard deviation	Average errors	Standard deviation	Average errors	Standard deviation
Major advanced economies	**0.3**	**1.2**	**0.2**	**1.1**	**—**	**0.6**	**—**	**0.4**
United States	−0.5	1.7	−0.4	1.6	−0.2	0.8	−0.1	0.7
Japan	1.4	2.2	1.0	2.1	0.2	1.3	0.4	0.6
Germany	0.6	1.4	0.5	1.5	−0.1	1.0	−0.1	0.9
France	0.6	1.4	0.5	1.5	0.1	0.8	—	0.6
Italy	0.9	1.2	0.8	1.1	0.3	0.7	0.1	0.5
United Kingdom	0.5	1.8	0.4	1.7	−0.1	0.9	−0.2	0.4
Canada	0.5	1.9	0.4	1.8	0.2	1.1	0.1	0.7

[1]Forecast errors are defined as forecast minus outturn. Sample period covers 1990–2000.

time: (1) the May issue one year prior to the year in question; (2) the October issue one year prior to the year in question; (3) the May issue of the year in question; and (4) the October issue of the year in question. This methodology provides information on the accuracy of the *World Economic Outlook* growth forecasts at four different points in time leading up to the point when the growth outturn was realized. The sample of countries includes all member countries of the IMF, except the countries in transition (where forecast errors in the early part of the transition—a unique event—were very large, and would significantly bias the results).

The following points are worth noting:

- The average error for global growth is modestly positive for the one-year ahead forecasts, turning slightly negative in the current year forecast. The standard deviation of the global growth forecasts averages 0.9 percentage points in the one-year ahead forecast, falling to 0.3 to 0.5 percentage points in the current year.[3] Unsurprisingly, across almost all regions, the average forecast error (in absolute value) and the standard deviation declined the shorter the forecast period.

- The moderate overestimation of growth in world output in the one-year ahead forecast stems largely from the forecast errors in the advanced economies, most of which are associ-

[3]Implying that the forecast was within these intervals over two-thirds of the time.

ated with turning points. This was due to an underestimation of the extent of the recessions in the United States, Canada, and the United Kingdom in 1991; the euro area in 1993; and Japan during 1992–95 and 1997–99. Offsetting this positive error to some degree was an underestimation of growth in the United States in the second half of the 1990s, a period of surprisingly rapid productivity growth.

- As can be seen from the second table, the mean and standard deviation of the errors in the *World Economic Outlook* forecast for Group of Seven (G-7) countries are similar to those of private forecasters. While the average error of the consensus forecasts for most G-7 countries was slightly smaller for the one-year ahead forecasts compared to the *World Economic Outlook* forecasts, the standard deviation of the consensus forecast error was slightly higher. A more detailed comparison of consensus forecasts, *World Economic Outlook* forecasts, and OECD forecasts finds a high degree of similarity among all three, and concludes that it is difficult to say unambiguously which one is better (Loungani, 2000).

- For developing countries in the first table, the overall bias to the projections is generally small, but the forecasting experience differs significantly across regions, largely reflecting the differing shocks that each faced.

In *Africa*, the average forecasting error was significantly positive for the period (and in every individual year); in part this arises from the obvious difficulties in predicting conflicts and natural disasters that have seriously affected growth during the decade, as well as a possible tendency to overestimate growth in the context of IMF programs.[4] Also, for many African countries, data are available with a longer lag and are subject to larger revisions than those for other countries.

In *developing Asia,* growth was on average underestimated, entirely reflecting an underestimation of growth in China (which has a large weight in the aggregate) during the overheating period in the first half of the 1990s. This was offset in part by an overestimation of growth in the ASEAN-4, primarily during the Asian Crisis in 1997 and 1998 (which also accounts for the very large standard deviation in the forecast for this group).

In the *Middle East,* the one-year ahead forecasts overestimated growth in the 1990s, mainly reflecting an overestimation of the speed of recovery from the Gulf War.

In the *Western Hemisphere,* the average error for the one-year ahead growth forecast growth was positive, mainly reflecting an overestima-

tion of growth during the Mexican crisis in 1995 and the Brazil crisis in 1998–99. In the current year, however, forecast errors have been slightly negative, mainly reflecting an underestimation of pickups in Argentina and Brazil.

In conclusion, the above analysis suggests that, excluding the transition economies, the IMF's global growth forecasts have been relatively unbiased over the past decade. However, the experience varies substantially across regions, generally reflecting the particular shocks they have experienced. In particular, like outside forecasters, IMF forecasters have not been particularly successful in capturing major turning points and the ensuing impact on activity. This is, of course, particularly relevant at the present juncture, and while this tendency was recognized while making the forecast, it remains a source of potential downside risk. It is also likely, in the present situation, that the uncertainty around the forecast is larger than historical values of the standard deviation would tend to suggest. In some cases, notably Africa, there is evidence of more persistent overestimation of growth, in part for the structural reasons described above, a tendency that needs to be kept in mind in interpreting the forecasts and drawing the appropriate policy conclusions.

---

[4] IMF forecasts assume that programs are implemented.

delay the recovery of household and business confidence and push deferred spending—especially on business investment and household durables—further into 2002 than currently envisaged. Such tendencies could be aggravated by the legacy of high levels of business investment in the late 1990s and high levels of household debt.

In Canada, the slowdown has been sharper than earlier envisaged, mainly reflecting events in the United States. Real GDP growth has slowed substantially since late 2000, with growth of 1.4 percent now expected in 2001 and 0.8 percent in 2002. Economic activity is expected to turn around starting in the first half of 2002 and gradually gather pace during the year—supported by

a similar strengthening of activity in the United States, easier monetary conditions (the Bank of Canada having lowered official interest rates by 3½ percentage points in 2001), fiscal stimulus stemming from the tax cuts legislated last year, and the workings of the automatic stabilizers. As elsewhere in the global economy, however, the heightened level of uncertainty makes the timing and pace of a rebound difficult to gauge.

Japan

The events of September 11 and their aftermath have exacerbated what was already a difficult and troubling economic situation in Japan.

Box 3.2. Fiscal Stimulus and the Outlook for the United States

Together with the substantial easing of monetary policy since January, the tax cuts enacted in June and emergency spending measures passed in the immediate aftermath of the September 11 attacks have ensured that a considerable stimulus is in the pipeline in the United States. These initiatives will provide $375 billion in fiscal stimulus over the 2002 to 2004 fiscal years (the 2002 U.S. fiscal year runs from October 2001 to September 2002; see the Table). This equals 1 percent of GDP for 2002 and nearly 1¼ percent of GDP in 2003 and 2004. The tax cuts enacted in June 2001 comprise $243 billion of the stimulus, while emergency spending authorized by Congress immediately following the September 11 terrorist attacks adds another $63 billion. This includes $38 billion for defense, $20 billion for disaster recovery, and $5 billion to aid the airline industry.

In addition, the Bush Administration has proposed a new fiscal stimulus package of $60 to $75 billion over fiscal years 2002 to 2004, while Congress is considering packages amounting to around $100 billion in fiscal year 2002 and around $210 billion total through 2004. The resulting stimulus could be smaller if the spending initiatives of $69 billion requested in the Administration's fiscal year 2002 Budget but not yet enacted were to be used instead to meet new spending requirements. Along with additional spending for national security expected to amount to around $50 billion over 2002 to 2004, a new fiscal package of $75 billion would result in a total fiscal stimulus during fiscal years 2002 to 2004 of around $500 billion, roughly 1½ percent of GDP for the period.

With a new fiscal package comprised of temporary measures, the unified budget in the United States is now expected to be slightly in deficit in FY 2002 after surpluses from 1998 to 2001. Most of the decline relates to the impact of the fiscal policy initiatives, although the operation of the automatic fiscal stabilizers also has an impact. The cumulative surplus would be reduced from around $2.4 trillion to $2.2 trillion in fiscal years 2002 to 2011—a fairly modest change, as U.S. growth is expected to rebound

Fiscal Stimulus Measures, Fiscal Years 2002 to 2004
(Billions of dollars for each fiscal year)

	2002	2003	2004	Total 2002–04
Total fiscal stimulus measures	176	184	140	500
(Percent of GDP)	1.7	1.7	1.2	1.5
Stimulus under current policies	100	137	138	375
Taxes				
2001 tax cut package	38	93	112	243
Spending				
Defense	22	16	1	38
Other	40	28	26	94
Additional stimulus	77	47	2	125
Taxes				
New fiscal stimulus package	60	15	0	75
Spending				
Defense	13	21	2	35
Other	4	12	0	15

Source: IMF Staff estimates. Columns may not sum to total due to rounding.

strongly after 2002. If tax measures in the new stimulus package were permanent rather than temporary, the cumulative budget surplus would fall to $1.3 trillion over the fiscal years 2002 to 2011. If economic growth turned out to be even weaker than forecast, a $75 billion temporary stimulus package would likely result in the cumulative budget surplus over fiscal years 2002 to 2011 falling to less than $1.0 trillion.

Assessment of a New Fiscal Stimulus Package

The economic and budgetary impact of a fiscal stimulus will depend crucially on the particular tax and spending initiatives enacted. The objective should be to structure a package that shores up consumer confidence and boosts activity, without unduly compromising the longer-term fiscal position.

Well-targeted spending increases are typically considered to have a larger multiplier impact on activity than tax reductions, and could thus yield a quick and effective boost to the economy. The Administration and Congress are considering such measures as extending the duration of unemployment insurance and providing grants to assist in financing health care coverage to unemployed workers and their families. While assistance to unemployed workers could help shore up confidence, there would likely be adverse effects on individuals' incentives to find employment, though this could be mitigated by ensuring that the assistance is explicitly temporary. A number of proposals are also being considered in the wake of the terrorist attacks to increase spending on transportation security and infrastructure, as well as other programs less obviously related to the events of September 11. As with any spending initiatives, the benefits of these programs must be weighed against long-term costs, including the possibility that a "piling on" of new programs could undermine fiscal discipline over the longer term, implying a permanently higher path of public spending.

Temporary income tax cuts would be likely to have only a limited near-term impact, unless they are targeted at "liquidity-constrained" individuals, who would have a higher propensity to spend such tax reductions. Corporate tax measures being considered—including the elimination of the corporate alternative minimum tax, and an increase in the carryback period for net operating income losses—would entail significant revenue losses, while potentially providing little short-term stimulus to the economy. Temporary incentives aimed at investment, such as proposed partial expensing of business investment (or accelerated depreciation) could be more useful in bringing forward private investment. Of course, reducing tax burdens can have salutary medium-term effects, and these measures should be considered in due course consistent with achieving medium-term fiscal objectives. Other measures under consideration include a reduction in the capital gains tax for individuals and an increase in the amount of capital losses that can be deducted from income. These proposals face the risk of a perverse effect of encouraging a sell-off in equities; the resulting decline in stock prices and household wealth would further affect consumption.

The "reversibility" of various policies is also an important consideration. Given the lags involved between the easing of fiscal and monetary policy and the impact on activity, it could become necessary to withdraw some of the stimulus as the U.S. economy rebounds. This would tend to favor using monetary policy for any further stimulus, since policy interest rates can be adjusted relatively rapidly. In contrast, in the event of a quick recovery in the middle of 2002, institutional and political considerations might make it more difficult to withdraw fiscal stimulus within the timeframe needed to avoid overheating. Among the risks would be that permanent tax measures that have a significantly adverse impact on the U.S. debt profile could lead to higher long-term interest rates and thus offset the stimulus from a shorter-lived policy. Looking forward, it will be important as well to take offsetting action by either tax or expenditure measures when the economy recovers so that the United States can achieve its medium-term objective of saving the surplus in the Social Security trust fund in order to begin dealing with the challenges associated with the aging of the U.S. population.

Household and business confidence have fallen further in recent months, while business conditions have continued to weaken—especially in the manufacturing sector, where indicators of excess capacity, employment, and inventories have all deteriorated. Weaker economic prospects and persistently low equity prices have added to concerns about financial system stability, particularly in view of writedowns in bank capital under mark-to-market accounting rules and uncertainties about the full extent of non-performing loans.[1] The steep downturn in ex-

---

[1]Mark-to-market accounting rules came into effect at the beginning of April 2001 and are reflected for the first time in financial results for the half year ending in September 2001.

ports since 2000 also looks set to continue, especially given the prospect of delayed recoveries in the United States and Asia and the ongoing weakness in the global electronics market.

Reflecting these developments, the modest recovery that had been projected to emerge early in 2002 is now not expected until at least the second half of the year. In 2002 as a whole, the economy is expected to contract by 1 percent, accompanied by ongoing deflation. A high level of uncertainty and risk—predominantly on the downside—surrounds even this bleak outlook. A key concern is of a vicious cycle involving weakening growth, rising numbers of corporate bankruptcies, and increasing concerns about the health of the banking sector. With a gradual pickup later in 2002 expected to be driven by the external sector, greater-than-expected weakness in the global economy or a depreciation of the dollar against the yen—for example, as a result of heightened economic or security concerns in the United States—would imply additional downside risks for Japan.

The prospect of continuing and possibly intensified weakness in the Japanese economy highlights even more forcefully than before the need to implement an ambitious and coordinated strategy to tackle deep-seated economic weaknesses. This strategy has two key elements. First, persistent weaknesses in the banking sector need to be addressed, particularly through stronger loan classification and provisioning practices, disposal of nonperforming loans, and, where appropriate, targeted use of public funds through mechanisms that lead to substantive restructuring of the institutions involved.[2] In addition, corporate restructuring should be accelerated, with banks continuing to take the lead in restructuring their potentially viable borrowers, but under stronger incentives and clearer timetables for achieving results. Second, macroeconomic policies need to be supportive of this strategy, to help offset potential short-term impacts of structural reforms on real activity and to counteract defla-

tionary pressures. In particular, a more ambitious monetary response is required: the Bank of Japan needs to make a clear commitment to end deflation within a reasonable timeframe and support this by further quantitative easing, even if such a policy were to result in some further depreciation of the yen. On the fiscal side, with near-term economic prospects weakening, the second supplementary budget will go a significant way toward avoiding a withdrawal of stimulus in 2002, and thereby reduce downside risks to activity. The budget will focus on priorities of the government that will aid structural reform, including public works spending on urban regeneration, information technology, and support for the elderly. At the same time, however, the authorities need to push ahead with measures that will support fiscal consolidation over the medium term, including health sector reforms and ending the earmarking of tax revenues.

Euro Area

Economic prospects in the euro area have also deteriorated over recent months, with the events of September 11 hitting economies that were already slowing as a result of regional and global shocks—including higher oil and food prices, the reassessment of the technology and telecommunications sectors, and the associated fall in equity prices. Indicators of industrial production, service sector activity, and business confidence have weakened throughout the area. The widely-followed IFO business confidence indicator in Germany has fallen to its lowest level since 1993, while the declines elsewhere have been less stark. Other leading indicators of business conditions have yet to show a turning point, making the timing of recovery uncertain. The fall in global confidence and activity is also significant, given the importance of trade and other international economic and financial linkages. For example, the large share of trade between the United States and Europe taking place between subsidiaries of multinational companies

---

[2]An emergency account amounting to 15 trillion yen is available to ensure the stability of the financial system in case of systemic threat.

(such "related party trade" accounted for around 65 percent of all U.S. imports from Germany in 2000) may tend to strengthen the balance sheet linkages associated with this trade channel. Consumer confidence has also been declining, probably reflecting international linkages in sentiment together with weak real income growth and rising unemployment, and appears likely to stay under pressure as a result of the increase in domestic and global uncertainty.

As a result, GDP growth for the euro area in 2002 is now projected at 1.2 percent, 1 percentage point lower than projected in October. Part of this downward revision reflects the carryover effect on growth in 2002 from recent data indicating growth was weakening even before September 11. Among the largest economies, the weakness in Germany—where growth is expected to be only 0.7 percent in 2002—is particularly marked and, given the strong economic linkages within Europe, will adversely affect growth in the region.[3] Growth in France and Italy is expected to be 1.2 to 1.3 percent in 2002, also well below potential.

A number of influences should tend to support activity in the period ahead. Inflation is expected to continue falling, particularly in response to lower energy and food prices, and this should help to unwind some of the downward pressures on real incomes and spending that were evident earlier in the year. Support for export activity should come from the continued favorable exchange rate for the euro. On the policy side, the European Central Bank has lowered official rates by 1½ percentage points since the beginning of the year, including 1 percentage point since September 11, and with inflationary pressures weakening there will be room for additional easing if necessary. With fiscal policy, the automatic stabilizers should be allowed to operate across the euro area but, beyond this, the scope for additional support varies across countries. Earlier tax reductions in Germany and France should continue to provide support to demand, and modest tax cuts are to occur in

Italy in 2002. These countries though have little additional room for maneuver on the fiscal front, given the 3 percent deficit ceiling under the Stability and Growth Pact, and the only limited progress made in improving structural fiscal balances during the recent period of relatively strong growth (Table 3.2). Other countries, including Ireland, Finland, Netherlands, and Spain, appear to have greater scope for a cautious easing of fiscal policy if downward pressures on activity prevail.

More generally, while the euro area has less policy stimulus in the pipeline than the United States, it also appears less vulnerable in some respects than the United States to adverse shocks to confidence and activity: external balances are stronger; households are less indebted and less exposed to stock market developments; and concerns about overinvestment and overcapacity among firms appear to be lower. But, to underpin a robust recovery, it is critical—both for Europe and for the rest of the world—that such strengths are complemented by more aggressive structural reforms to labor, product and financial markets, and other areas that have been holding down Europe's potential growth rate and contributing, at least indirectly, to broader imbalances in the global economy. The historic introduction of euro notes and coins, beginning January 1, 2002, will further strengthen European integration and support the structural reform process—for example, by increasing the transparency of price differences within the euro area and reducing the costs of cross-border transactions.

As in other advanced economies, the prospective depth and duration of the downturn in household and business confidence represent a key uncertainty in the current outlook. While recovery could start earlier than envisaged, the key policy concern is clearly that of a more prolonged downturn. In addition to the impact of the global slowdown and of increased international tensions, a particular concern in Europe stems from the weaker labor market outlook—with unemployment again increasing from al-

[3]See Box 1.5 in the October 2001 *World Economic Outlook.*

Table 3.2. Major Advanced Economies: General Government Fiscal Balances and Debt[1]
(Percent of GDP)

	1985–94	1995	1996	1997	1998	1999	2000	2001	2002	2006
Major advanced economies										
Actual balance	−3.7	−4.1	−3.4	−2.0	−1.4	−1.1	−0.2	−1.3	−1.8	0.2
Output gap[2]	−0.5	−2.2	−2.0	−1.4	−1.2	−0.8	—	−1.4	−3.2	−0.2
Structural balance	−3.4	−3.2	−2.6	−1.3	−0.8	−0.7	−0.6	−0.8	−0.6	0.2
United States										
Actual balance	−4.7	−3.3	−2.4	−1.3	−0.1	0.6	1.5	0.3	−0.5	0.9
Output gap[2]	−1.3	−3.2	−2.8	−1.6	−0.5	0.4	1.4	−0.8	−3.1	—
Structural balance	−4.2	−2.3	−1.5	−0.7	0.1	0.5	1.0	0.5	0.5	0.9
Net debt	51.4	59.6	59.2	57.0	53.4	48.9	43.7	42.0	41.3	30.2
Gross debt	65.7	72.9	72.8	70.3	66.6	63.4	57.4	55.2	54.2	40.3
Japan										
Actual balance	0.6	−3.5	−4.2	−3.2	−4.5	−6.8	−7.9	−7.2	−7.1	−1.4
Excluding social security	−2.5	−6.3	−6.7	−5.8	−6.5	−8.6	−9.2	−7.9	−7.5	−2.4
Output gap[2]	1.1	−1.3	0.5	0.3	−2.4	−3.2	−2.5	−4.1	−6.2	−0.9
Structural balance	0.3	−3.2	−4.3	−3.4	−3.6	−5.8	−7.0	−5.6	−4.7	−1.2
Excluding social security	−2.9	−6.0	−6.9	−5.9	−6.0	−8.0	−8.7	−7.1	−6.2	−2.4
Net debt	13.5	12.7	16.0	17.5	29.5	35.8	42.9	50.1	57.7	61.7
Gross debt	70.6	87.1	92.4	96.9	110.2	120.3	129.7	140.8	152.5	153.5
Euro area										
Actual balance	−4.7	−5.0	−4.3	−2.6	−2.2	−1.3	0.2	−1.1	−1.4	0.1
Output gap[2]	−0.3	−1.2	−1.9	−1.8	−1.2	−1.0	−0.1	−0.9	−2.1	−0.2
Structural balance	. . .	−4.1	−3.0	−1.4	−1.3	−0.7	−0.7	−0.8	−0.6	0.1
Net debt	43.8	60.6	62.4	62.8	61.3	60.4	58.2	57.4	57.1	49.8
Gross debt	59.4	73.3	75.5	75.3	73.6	72.6	70.2	68.9	68.6	59.5
Germany[3]										
Actual balance[4]	−1.9	−3.3	−3.4	−2.7	−2.2	−1.6	1.2	−2.5	−2.5	—
Output gap[2]	−0.2	0.4	−0.7	−1.2	−1.1	−1.1	—	−1.2	−2.4	—
Structural balance	−1.5	−3.4	−2.8	−1.7	−1.3	−0.8	−1.3	−1.8	−1.2	—
Net debt	24.9	49.4	51.1	52.2	52.0	52.4	51.6	51.1	52.1	45.5
Gross debt	43.8	58.3	59.8	60.9	60.7	61.1	60.3	59.8	60.8	54.2
France										
Actual balance[4]	−3.3	−5.5	−4.1	−3.0	−2.7	−1.6	−1.4	−0.9	−2.1	—
Output gap[2]	−0.3	−2.7	−3.3	−3.1	−1.8	−1.2	−0.2	−0.6	−1.7	—
Structural balance	−2.9	−3.7	−1.9	−1.0	−1.5	−0.9	−1.2	−1.2	−1.4	—
Net debt	28.3	45.8	48.1	49.6	49.8	48.9	47.9	48.8	48.2	43.8
Gross debt	36.9	54.6	57.1	59.3	59.5	58.5	57.5	57.0	57.9	53.5
Italy										
Actual balance[4,5]	−10.5	−7.6	−7.1	−2.7	−2.8	−1.8	−0.3	−1.2	−1.0	−0.5
Output gap[2]	−0.1	−1.1	−2.0	−2.3	−2.4	−2.7	−1.8	−1.9	−2.6	—
Structural balance	−10.4	−7.0	−6.2	−1.7	−1.8	−0.6	−0.7	−0.5	−0.6	−0.5
Net debt	93.2	116.6	116.0	113.7	110.1	108.4	104.4	102.3	101.6	90.0
Gross debt	99.5	123.2	122.6	120.1	116.2	114.5	110.2	108.0	107.3	95.2
United Kingdom										
Actual balance[4]	−3.2	−5.4	−4.1	−1.5	0.3	1.5	3.9	0.5	−0.1	−0.8
Output gap[2]	0.4	−1.1	−1.3	−0.5	0.2	−0.5	0.1	—	−0.9	—
Structural balance	−2.5	−4.6	−3.3	−0.9	0.5	1.5	1.7	0.5	0.1	−0.7
Net debt	26.5	36.8	46.2	44.6	41.9	39.0	34.3	31.3	30.1	28.0
Gross debt	43.4	51.7	51.8	49.6	46.5	43.9	40.7	38.3	37.0	33.5
Canada										
Actual balance	−6.9	−5.3	−2.8	0.2	0.5	1.6	3.2	1.9	1.0	1.1
Output gap[2]	−1.8	−5.5	−6.5	−5.1	−3.9	−1.7	−0.1	−1.4	−3.2	—
Structural balance	−5.6	−2.8	—	2.1	2.5	2.5	3.3	2.6	2.7	1.1
Net debt	66.3	88.6	87.8	84.1	81.2	74.9	66.3	61.5	59.5	44.0
Gross debt	98.0	120.4	120.3	117.6	115.7	112.3	102.6	97.4	94.9	72.6

[1]Debt data refer to end of year; for the United Kingdom they refer to end of March.
[2]Percent of potential.
[3]Data before 1990 refer to west Germany. For net debt, the first column refers to 1988–94. Beginning in 1995, the debt and debt-service obligations of the Treuhandanstalt (and of various other agencies) were taken over by general government. This debt is equivalent to 8 percent of GDP, and the associated debt service to ½ to 1 percent of GDP.
[4]Includes one-off receipts from the sale of mobile telephone licenses equivalent to 2.5 percent of GDP in 2000 for Germany, 0.5 percent of GDP in 2001 for France, 1.2 percent of GDP in 2000 for Italy, and 2.4 percent of GDP in 2000 for the United Kingdom.
[5]Includes asset sales equivalent to 0.2 percent of GDP in 2001, 0.7 percent in 2002, 0.5 percent in 2003, and 0.1 percent in 2004.

ready high levels in the largest euro area economies. In addition, a further decline in economic prospects could lead to renewed weakness in stock prices, which are already down significantly since the beginning of the year. Although the significance of equity holdings differs among euro area economies, and as noted above is generally lower than in the United States, such a fall would add to downward pressures on household demand and on business investment spending.

Other Advanced Economies

The outlook for other advanced economies has also deteriorated, driven by the weakening prospects for trade and declining business and consumer confidence, but with important country-by-country differences. In the United Kingdom, economic activity has so far been more resilient to the global downturn than activity in other major advanced economies. Industrial output has continued to fall while exports weakened in the second quarter, influenced mainly by the shocks to the information technology (IT) sector and also by the strong exchange rate. Demand has been buoyed by strong private consumption growth and by already budgeted increases in government spending. However, the recent softening of business and consumer confidence as well as house prices and labor market indicators suggest that private consumption growth is likely to slow down. Reflecting this, growth projected for 2002 has been marked down to 1.8 percent (compared with 2.4 percent in the last *World Economic Outlook*). The Bank of England has lowered interest rates by 1 percentage point since the terrorist attacks and, provided the inflation outlook remains benign, there would be scope for further reductions if economic prospects deteriorate more than currently envisaged.

The 2002 outlook for the smaller European economies outside the euro area has also been marked down by varying degrees—by 0.3 points in Denmark and Norway, and 0.8 to 0.9 points in Sweden and Switzerland. In addition to poorer export market conditions in Europe and falling domestic confidence, these countries also face

some more specific pressures. Norway, for example, is exposed to oil market developments; Switzerland has experienced some currency appreciation stemming from safe haven related capital inflows following September 11; and Sweden has faced persistent weakness in the krona, which should provide some support to exports. How these pressures unfold, together with the outlook for inflation and output more broadly, will determine the scope for further easings in monetary policy—each of these countries having already lowered interest rates in the aftermath of September 11.

Elsewhere, economic conditions in Australia and to a lesser extent New Zealand appear reasonably robust despite some recent weakening in confidence. Growth in Australia in 2002 is expected to reach 3.3 percent, stronger than in 2001 although ½ of a percentage point lower than projected in the October *World Economic Outlook*, while growth in New Zealand is projected to weaken somewhat to 1.9 percent. Export performance has been well-sustained in both countries in 2001—helped by weak currencies and, in New Zealand, by more favorable agricultural growing conditions—and this has contributed to sharp reductions in their current account deficits. External performance could still come under pressure, however, if global growth and commodity prices remain weak. Household spending has also held up quite well: house construction is up strongly in Australia, supported by lower interest rates and earlier homeowner incentives; and lower interest rates, rising rural incomes, and continued low unemployment are contributing to the resilience of demand in New Zealand.

Emerging Markets

Developing and transition economies are being hit on several fronts by the events of September 11 and their aftermath, with the result that projections for almost all regions have been marked down from those in the October *World Economic Outlook* (Table 3.3). This weaker outlook stems from several interrelated influ-

Table 3.3. Selected Developing and Transition Economies: Real GDP, Consumer Prices, and Current Account Balance

(Annual percent change unless otherwise noted)

	Real GDP				Consumer Prices[1]				Current Account Balance[2]			
	1999	2000	2001	2002	1999	2000	2001	2002	1999	2000	2001	2002
Developing countries	**3.9**	**5.8**	**4.0**	**4.4**	**6.8**	**5.9**	**6.0**	**5.3**	**−0.2**	**1.1**	**0.1**	**−1.2**
Africa	**2.5**	**2.8**	**3.5**	**3.5**	**11.6**	**13.5**	**12.8**	**8.3**	**−3.6**	**0.9**	**−0.8**	**−3.3**
Algeria	3.2	2.4	3.6	3.4	2.6	0.3	3.7	5.2	—	16.8	11.1	0.6
Ghana	4.4	3.7	4.0	4.0	12.4	25.2	33.0	15.9	−11.5	−9.1	−7.9	−5.8
Kenya	1.3	−0.2	1.1	1.4	6.1	7.1	5.0	5.0	−2.2	−2.1	−2.9	−4.0
Morocco	−0.7	0.8	6.1	4.4	0.7	1.9	2.5	2.3	−0.5	−1.7	−1.4	−0.4
Nigeria	1.1	3.8	4.2	1.8	6.6	6.9	19.3	15.2	−9.5	4.8	−4.1	−10.6
Tunisia	6.1	4.7	5.4	5.3	2.7	2.9	2.9	2.7	−2.1	−4.2	−4.2	−3.9
South Africa	1.9	3.1	2.2	2.3	5.2	5.4	5.8	4.5	−0.4	−0.3	0.5	1.0
Developing Asia	**6.2**	**6.8**	**5.6**	**5.6**	**2.5**	**1.9**	**2.8**	**3.0**	**2.2**	**2.1**	**1.1**	**0.2**
Bangladesh	5.4	6.0	4.7	3.2	6.4	2.3	1.8	4.0	−1.4	−1.6	−2.4	−2.4
China	7.1	8.0	7.3	6.8	−1.4	0.4	1.0	1.0	1.6	1.9	1.0	0.3
India	6.8	6.0	4.4	5.2	4.7	4.0	3.9	4.8	−0.7	−0.9	−0.6	−0.7
Indonesia	0.8	4.8	3.2	3.5	20.7	3.8	11.5	10.9	4.1	5.2	3.4	1.0
Malaysia	6.1	8.3	0.3	2.5	2.8	1.5	1.5	1.8	15.9	9.4	7.5	5.1
Pakistan	4.1	3.9	3.7	4.4	4.1	4.4	3.8	5.0	−2.8	−1.9	−2.1	−2.2
Philippines	3.4	4.0	2.9	3.2	6.6	4.3	6.1	5.0	10.0	12.1	4.9	2.8
Thailand	4.3	4.4	1.5	2.0	0.3	1.5	1.7	1.1	10.2	7.5	4.7	4.0
Vietnam	4.2	5.5	4.7	4.8	4.1	−1.7	0.8	4.9	4.5	2.1	1.7	−1.1
Middle East[3]	**3.0**	**5.5**	**4.5**	**3.8**	**12.1**	**9.2**	**9.4**	**9.0**	**3.0**	**11.6**	**6.0**	**−0.6**
Egypt	6.0	5.1	3.3	3.3	3.8	2.8	2.4	3.0	−1.9	−1.2	—	−1.6
Iran, Islamic Rep. of	3.1	5.8	5.0	4.8	20.4	12.6	16.0	13.0	6.4	13.0	4.1	1.6
Saudi Arabia	−0.8	4.5	2.3	1.6	−1.3	−0.6	−1.1	1.4	0.3	9.0	4.0	−6.4
Western Hemisphere	**0.1**	**4.1**	**1.0**	**1.7**	**8.8**	**8.1**	**6.3**	**5.2**	**−3.2**	**−2.5**	**−3.0**	**−2.9**
Argentina	−3.4	−0.5	−2.7	−1.1	−1.2	−0.9	−1.0	−0.5	−4.2	−3.2	−2.4	−1.2
Brazil	0.5	4.4	1.8	2.0	4.9	7.0	6.7	5.6	−4.8	−4.1	−4.7	−4.0
Chile	−1.1	5.4	3.3	3.0	3.3	3.8	3.7	3.3	−0.1	−1.4	−2.0	−1.9
Colombia	−4.1	2.8	1.4	2.4	10.9	9.2	8.0	7.6	0.2	0.4	−2.6	−3.4
Ecuador	−7.3	2.3	5.2	3.8	52.2	96.2	37.0	8.8	6.9	5.3	−4.6	−4.4
Mexico	3.7	6.9	—	1.2	16.6	9.5	6.5	5.0	−3.0	−3.2	−3.0	−3.5
Peru	0.9	3.1	0.2	3.7	3.5	3.8	2.1	1.8	−3.8	−3.1	−2.1	−2.3
Venezuela	−6.1	3.2	2.7	1.8	23.6	16.2	12.6	13.5	3.6	10.8	4.3	2.7
E.U. accession candidates	**—**	**4.8**	**0.2**	**3.4**	**25.3**	**24.4**	**21.5**	**18.1**	**−4.1**	**−5.2**	**−3.0**	**−3.9**
Bulgaria	2.4	5.8	4.5	3.8	2.6	10.4	7.2	4.2	−5.3	−5.8	−7.1	−5.7
Czech Republic	−0.4	2.9	3.3	3.1	2.1	4.0	3.9	3.8	−2.9	−4.8	−5.5	−5.2
Estonia	−0.7	6.9	4.5	4.1	3.3	4.0	5.7	3.0	−4.7	−6.4	−6.8	−6.8
Hungary	4.5	5.2	3.7	3.5	10.0	9.8	9.2	5.5	−4.3	−3.3	−2.2	−2.6
Latvia	1.1	6.6	7.0	4.5	2.4	2.6	2.5	3.0	−9.8	−6.9	−7.1	−7.0
Lithuania	−3.9	3.9	3.9	4.3	0.8	1.0	1.4	2.2	−11.2	−6.0	−6.0	−5.8
Poland	4.1	4.1	1.5	2.2	7.3	10.1	5.7	5.1	−7.5	−6.3	−4.0	−4.3
Romania	−2.3	1.6	4.8	4.6	45.8	45.7	34.1	25.9	−4.1	−3.7	−6.0	−5.6
Slovak Republic	1.9	2.2	2.7	3.1	10.7	12.0	7.5	4.1	−5.7	−3.7	−8.6	−7.7
Slovenia	5.2	4.6	3.0	3.0	6.2	8.5	6.5	6.0	−3.9	−3.2	−1.1	−2.5
Turkey	−4.7	7.2	−6.1	4.1	64.9	54.9	53.9	46.4	−0.7	−4.9	1.6	−1.4
Commonwealth of Independent States	**4.6**	**7.9**	**6.1**	**3.9**	**70.6**	**25.0**	**20.6**	**13.5**	**7.3**	**13.5**	**8.1**	**3.4**
Belarus	3.4	5.9	3.0	1.5	293.8	169.0	61.0	26.0	−1.6	−1.3	1.6	−0.4
Kazakhstan	2.8	9.4	9.0	7.0	8.4	13.3	8.5	7.0	−1.0	4.3	−4.7	−6.1
Russia	5.4	8.3	5.8	3.6	85.7	20.8	21.5	14.0	11.8	18.0	11.0	5.6
Ukraine	−0.2	5.8	8.2	5.0	22.7	28.2	11.9	9.0	2.6	4.7	3.0	1.2

[1]In accordance with standard practice in the *World Economic Outlook,* movements in consumer prices are indicated as annual averages rather than as December/December changes during the year, as is the practice in some countries.
[2]Percent of GDP.
[3]Includes Bahrain, Egypt, Islamic Rep. of Iran, Iraq, Jordan, Kuwait, Lebanon, Libya, Oman, Qatar, Saudi Arabia, Syrian Arab Republic, United Arab Emirates, and Republic of Yemen.

ences: the further slowing now expected in the advanced economies and spillover effects on trade and confidence; the particularly strong impact of the slowdown on some sectors—notably information technology and tourism—to which some emerging markets are heavily exposed; financial market linkages with advanced economies, especially in view of increased market uncertainties and deterioration in external financing conditions since September 11; and downward pressures on prices of fuel and nonfuel commodities, many of which were already weak.

The relative significance of these channels varies from region to region, although they all tend to be relevant to some degree. Asia, for example, will probably be strongly affected through the trade channel, with both export prices and volumes shown to be sensitive to the advanced economy cycle.[4] Compounding this linkage is the heavy exposure of many Asian economies to the severe downturn in the global electronics cycle, and some will also be hit by the downturn in tourism. Trade ties are also a key determinant of the outlook elsewhere: for example, the steeper slowdown in the United States will weaken further the outlook for Mexico and other countries in Central America; and countries in Central Europe and the Baltics will be hurt by the rapid slowing in Western Europe.

The sharp reactions of advanced economy financial markets to the September 11 attacks were echoed and amplified in emerging markets, with falling stock prices, widening bond spreads, and weakening currencies. While these trends have subsequently reversed in many emerging market economies, countries with substantial external financing requirements remain vulnerable to potential reassessments of global or domestic economic prospects and to further shocks to international financial markets. These concerns are probably the strongest in Latin America—notably in Argentina, which is experiencing renewed financial turbulence, but also in

other regional economies with persistently high current account deficits and large external debts. There have also been heightened concerns regarding the outlook for Turkey, where the exchange rate fell substantially in September and early October, although it has subsequently strengthened. The economies of Central and Eastern Europe and the Baltics could potentially be at risk from adverse developments in global financial markets, given the rather high current account deficits in most of these countries; however, indications so far suggest that they are attracting funding without significant difficulty, possibly reflecting increased discrimination among investors toward countries with stronger economic fundamentals.

Recent commodity price developments will have the most direct and sizable impact in the Middle East, among the Commonwealth of Independent States (CIS), and in Africa, where many countries are heavily dependent on a narrow base of fuel or nonfuel commodity exports. As discussed below, growth and current account prospects for 2002 have weakened among most oil exporters, although in some cases—including Russia—significant carryover effects from strong growth in 2001 are still present. Lower oil prices will also have an adverse impact on a number of emerging market debtor countries, including Indonesia and Venezuela. The growth outlook for many African economies is expected to be held back by falling prices of almost all nonfuel commodities, some of which—notably coffee and cotton—were already at very depressed levels, although the impact will be partly offset by the lower price of oil imports.

In the following sections, countries and regions are broadly grouped according to three themes: those most exposed to weaker external demand, those with large external financing requirements, and those highly dependent on commodity exports. It should be stressed, however, that these influences are interrelated to some degree and most regions will be affected by more than one; as a result, regional distinc-

---

[4]See Chapter II of the October 2001 *World Economic Outlook* for analysis of these linkages.

tions are not clear-cut. Moreover, the impact of these pressures is not necessarily symmetric across the regions concerned—for example, deteriorating external financing conditions may have much more serious consequences for emerging market borrowers with weak fiscal and structural conditions than for those borrowers whose fundamentals are strong.

The Impact of Weakening External Demand

Weaker global growth is hampering the trade-dependent economies of Asia and Central America, the latter particularly influenced by the U.S. slowdown. In Asia, the marked weakening in the newly industrialized and ASEAN economies was driven initially by external influences—especially by lower growth in the United States and Europe, economic contraction in Japan, and the decline in the global electronics cycle (Figure 3.2). Particularly in a number of the newly industrialized economies, these pressures now appear to have been stronger than earlier thought, and have generally intensified since September 11. Furthermore, the slowdown has spread increasingly into domestic demand and into a broader range of nonelectronics and service sectors, including the tourism sector—of particular importance for Hong Kong SAR, Singapore, Thailand, and for a number of small island nations in the Asia-Pacific region.

In response to the slowdown, macroeconomic policies across the region have generally been eased. Most countries have lowered official interest rates since September 11, continuing the trend established before this date, and the weakening of most regional currencies (apart from those with fixed pegs) has also contributed to an easing of monetary conditions. In countries with low inflation and flexible exchange rates—such as Korea, Singapore, and Taiwan Province of China—there is still room for maneuver on the monetary front if necessary. On the fiscal side, the scope for adjustment varies considerably. Following widespread easing of fiscal policy earlier in the year, some countries—

Figure 3.2. Technology and Total Exports in Emerging Asia

Asian export growth has fallen significantly in 2001, largely as a result of the downturn in the global electronics cycle.

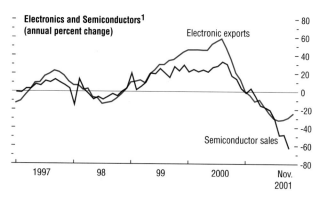

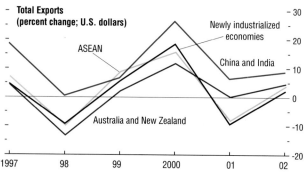

Source: IMF staff estimates.
[1] Three-month moving averages of 12-month percent change.

including Hong Kong SAR, Malaysia, and Singapore—have eased further in recent months, and there remains room for stimulus in Korea and other countries with low public debt. But high public debt or deficits in some cases—particularly in India, Indonesia, and the Philippines—greatly constrain the scope for further fiscal support.

Reflecting the greater-than-expected slowing in external demand and the weakness evident in sectors of domestic activity, growth projections across Asia have been revised down from those in the October 2001 *World Economic Outlook,* with recovery delayed into 2002. The sharpest reductions are in the outlook for the newly industrialized economies: Hong Kong SAR, Singapore, and Taiwan Province of China are now expected to grow by only around 1 percent in 2002, while firmer growth of 3¼ percent is projected for Korea. Growth in the ASEAN economies is projected to reach just under 3 percent in 2002, with the outlook for Malaysia (which in addition has been hit by lower oil revenues) and Thailand much weaker than anticipated in October. Activity is expected to hold up relatively well in China, where growth of close to 7 percent is projected for 2002, and in south Asia, including India and Pakistan, where growth of 4½ to 5 percent is expected. The more robust activity among these countries reflects the fact that they are less exposed, although not completely immune, to the downturn in global trade and activity compared with most of the smaller Asian economies. The prospective winding down of the conflict in Afghanistan and provision of large-scale international assistance for recovery should contribute significantly to growth in that country and may also boost activity in the surrounding region.

The key uncertainty in the outlook for much of Asia is the strength of export demand—especially the pace of recovery in technology sectors—but there are also concerns about a broader-based deterioration in domestic activity and confidence. Further risks could arise from financial sector weakness in some countries, including Indonesia, Taiwan Province of China,

and Thailand. More generally, the deterioration in external financing conditions since September 11 could affect capital flows, including direct investment, to Asia and other emerging markets—highlighting the importance of further structural reforms to strengthen financial and corporate sectors and hence to sustain external confidence. With still large current account surpluses and reserves, however, together with flexible exchange rates in many countries, Asia is relatively well placed to withstand external shocks. Lower world interest rates and lower oil prices should also help—although declining oil revenues will add to fiscal and external financing pressures in oil-exporting Indonesia.

The outlook for Central America and the Caribbean has been revised down sharply, largely reflecting the impact of weaker U.S. growth, falling remittances, and, for the Caribbean in particular, the downturn in tourism (see Box 3.3). The U.S. slowdown has led to a marked downturn of activity in Mexico, with growth of only 1¼ percent projected for 2002 compared with the 4 percent predicted in the October *World Economic Outlook.* However, the maintenance of firm fiscal and monetary policies has helped support investor confidence, as has the ongoing strengthening of the financial system. This has been reflected in the continued strength of the peso and a narrowing of bond spreads, following some weakening in the immediate aftermath of the September 11 attacks. The early passage of tax reform measures would further strengthen fiscal sustainability and flexibility over the medium term.

The smaller countries in Central America and the Caribbean are particularly vulnerable to recent developments. In Central America, exports to the United States account for almost 20 percent of GDP while, in the Caribbean, tourism accounts for 7 to 50 percent of GDP and by some estimates 25 percent of employment in the region (Box 3.3). Given the size of the external shock these countries are facing, domestic adjustment efforts—already under way in the Caribbean—will need to be complemented by additional external financing.

Table 3.4. Emerging Market Economies: Net Capital Flows[1]
(Billions of U.S. dollars)

	1993	1994	1995	1996	1997	1998	1999	2000	2001	2002
Total[2]										
Private capital flows, net[3]	145.6	151.3	205.7	233.2	116.8	69.6	59.6	8.9	20.1	59.8
Private direct investment, net	54.1	81.4	96.5	119.6	145.2	155.4	153.4	146.2	162.4	142.6
Private portfolio investment, net	87.6	113.1	41.2	86.9	48.6	−4.2	31.0	−4.3	−13.0	13.7
Other private capital flows, net	3.9	−43.2	68.0	26.8	−77.0	−81.6	−124.8	−133.0	−129.4	−96.6
Official flows, net	46.3	3.7	26.6	0.1	62.6	54.3	5.1	−3.6	34.2	21.4
Change in reserves[4]	−63.9	−69.9	−117.1	−109.4	−62.5	−45.2	−87.9	−114.2	−98.0	−34.4
Memorandum										
Current account[5]	−116.5	−72.6	−93.1	−95.5	−69.6	−53.2	37.8	128.9	51.5	−47.5
Africa										
Private capital flows, net[3]	2.5	13.4	11.5	11.1	8.4	10.0	11.9	7.0	9.5	10.0
Private direct investment, net	3.2	3.3	2.9	4.8	8.4	6.9	9.0	7.2	21.4	11.0
Private portfolio investment, net	0.9	3.5	3.1	2.8	7.0	3.7	8.7	−1.8	−6.3	4.2
Other private capital flows, net	−1.6	6.6	5.6	3.4	−6.9	−0.7	−5.8	1.6	−5.8	−5.2
Official flows, net	4.4	3.2	4.1	−0.2	1.3	2.6	0.4	−2.7	−0.2	0.7
Change in reserves[4]	2.8	−5.8	−2.0	−9.5	−11.3	0.7	−4.3	−14.8	−11.2	−2.0
Memorandum										
Current account[5]	−11.1	−11.5	−16.6	−5.1	−7.0	−20.0	−15.4	3.8	−3.6	−14.2
Developing Asia[6]										
Crisis countries[7]										
Private capital flows, net[3]	30.8	35.0	55.2	74.1	−5.9	−31.9	−18.3	−20.9	−24.1	−10.5
Private direct investment, net	6.7	6.5	10.3	11.7	10.2	11.4	8.9	5.1	1.8	4.8
Private portfolio investment, net	25.0	13.3	18.6	27.6	8.8	−9.0	13.1	7.0	−0.9	2.6
Other private capital flows, net	−0.8	15.2	26.3	34.8	−25.0	−34.3	−40.3	−32.9	−25.0	−18.0
Official flows, net	3.2	1.1	9.0	−4.5	14.1	17.3	−3.3	3.0	−0.2	−1.6
Change in reserves[4]	−20.0	−6.5	−17.3	−5.3	39.4	−46.9	−39.3	−23.8	−5.7	−5.9
Memorandum										
Current account[5]	−13.5	−23.2	−40.4	−53.0	−25.5	69.7	62.9	45.7	31.9	23.3
Other Asian emerging markets										
Private capital flows, net[3]	22.5	35.1	37.4	50.5	22.9	−13.0	9.7	4.9	17.2	6.0
Private direct investment, net	26.4	38.2	39.6	45.6	49.6	48.5	43.0	41.7	41.9	36.9
Private portfolio investment, net	0.9	7.5	2.1	3.5	−0.1	−6.3	0.7	−3.3	−3.8	1.2
Other private capital flows, net	−4.7	−10.6	−4.3	1.3	−26.6	−55.1	−34.1	−33.5	−21.0	−32.1
Official flows, net	8.2	2.5	−3.7	−7.9	−7.3	−0.3	2.1	−9.1	−1.9	3.6
Change in reserves[4]	−16.8	−51.6	−25.4	−41.6	−46.8	−16.9	−38.7	−26.2	−41.9	−23.7
Memorandum										
Current account[5]	−7.2	18.3	8.0	15.0	51.2	41.6	37.9	41.7	29.5	16.1
Memorandum										
Hong Kong SAR										
Private capital flows, net[3]	—	—	—	—	11.7	−8.5	1.0	3.8	8.3	1.4
Middle East, Malta, and Turkey[8]										
Private capital flows, net[3]	30.7	16.0	8.5	8.8	17.7	11.8	−1.1	−22.4	−29.2	−0.7
Private direct investment, net	3.2	5.2	6.4	4.7	5.2	6.3	5.4	7.2	6.5	8.4
Private portfolio investment, net	6.7	7.7	2.0	0.7	−0.9	−13.2	−4.2	−15.1	−9.6	−5.2
Other private capital flows, net	20.8	3.1	0.1	3.4	13.4	18.6	−2.3	−14.6	−26.1	−3.8
Official flows, net	1.7	3.4	4.4	6.5	7.8	1.8	−1.0	−0.6	10.6	0.9
Change in reserves[4]	1.6	−4.7	−11.3	−22.0	−20.5	10.6	−6.2	−25.3	−13.4	8.9
Memorandum										
Current account[5]	−30.8	−6.3	−5.3	4.9	2.6	−24.7	11.4	59.4	39.3	−6.7
Western Hemisphere										
Private capital flows, net[3]	39.3	47.1	44.0	66.4	70.6	71.7	43.6	37.9	38.8	39.5
Private direct investment, net	8.7	22.8	24.2	40.3	56.1	60.7	63.8	62.5	64.1	50.0
Private portfolio investment, net	45.5	65.0	0.8	38.8	25.9	16.5	9.8	4.6	4.0	7.6
Other private capital flows, net	−14.8	−40.7	19.0	−12.7	−11.5	−5.5	−30.0	−29.2	−29.3	−18.0
Official flows, net	29.9	4.7	18.6	3.4	13.7	15.6	6.4	6.2	24.2	14.1
Change in reserves[4]	−20.7	4.0	−23.3	−29.0	−13.8	8.8	7.7	−2.9	−6.8	—
Memorandum										
Current account[5]	−46.0	−52.2	−36.5	−40.5	−67.1	−90.7	−56.9	−48.7	−56.0	−55.3

Table 3.4 *(concluded)*

	1993	1994	1995	1996	1997	1998	1999	2000	2001	2002
Countries in transition										
Private capital flows, net[3]	19.8	4.6	49.0	22.3	3.2	21.0	13.8	2.2	7.6	15.0
Private direct investment, net	6.0	5.3	13.1	12.4	15.6	21.6	23.4	22.5	26.7	31.5
Private portfolio investment, net	8.7	16.1	14.6	13.4	8.0	4.0	2.8	4.3	3.6	3.5
Other private capital flows, net	5.1	−16.8	21.3	−3.5	−20.4	−4.6	−12.4	−24.7	−22.7	−20.0
Official flows, net	−1.1	−11.2	−5.8	2.6	32.9	17.2	0.5	−0.4	1.1	3.0
Change in reserves[4]	−10.9	−5.3	−37.8	−2.0	−9.4	−1.6	−7.1	−21.5	−19.7	−12.5
Memorandum										
Current account[5]	−7.9	2.3	−2.2	−16.8	−23.9	−29.1	−2.1	27.0	13.2	−6.0
Memorandum										
Fuel										
Private capital flows, net[3]	25.4	19.4	23.0	−7.1	−18.1	−2.6	−23.4	−61.1	−41.4	−27.9
Nonfuel										
Private capital flows, net[3]	120.2	131.8	182.7	240.3	134.9	72.2	83.0	70.0	61.5	87.7

[1]Net capital flows comprise net direct investment, net portfolio investment, and other long- and short-term net investment flows, including official and private borrowing. Emerging markets include developing countries, countries in transition, Korea, Singapore, Taiwan Province of China, and Israel.

[2]Exludes Hong Kong SAR .

[3]Because of data limitations, "other net investment" may include some official flows.

[4]A minus sign indicates an increase.

[5]The sum of the current account balance, net private capital flows, net official flows, and the change in reserves equals, with the opposite sign, the sum of the capital account and errors and omissions.

[6]Includes Korea, Singapore, and Taiwan Province of China.

[7]Includes Indonesia, Korea, Malaysia, the Philippines, and Thailand.

[8]Includes Israel.

Countries with Substantial External Financing Requirements

The increased uncertainty in global financial markets since September 11 has added to already significant concerns about economic prospects for economies with sizable external financing requirements. These concerns have been most acute in Latin America—notably Argentina—given the particularly high level of external debt and external financing needs of this region (Table 3.4). Moreover, many of these countries face additional pressures: some will be hard hit by the downturn in commodity prices—especially oil and metals—and in tourism; and, more generally, they face weaker export markets and lower domestic confidence. As a result, growth projections for Latin America in 2002 have been sharply reduced compared with those in the October *World Economic Outlook*. The outlook for Turkey has similarly been marked down, largely reflecting increased financial market uncertainties, and Pakistan has also seen a large increase in its bond spread and external financing requirement in the aftermath of September 11.

But countries in Central and Eastern Europe and the Baltics, which continue to run generally high current account deficits, have appeared better able to weather these uncertainties and meet their financing needs and are expected to show relatively robust growth in 2002.

Economic developments in Latin America have been dominated by the financial crisis in Argentina, which in some respects has been brought to a head by the recent turbulence in global financial markets. As discussed in Box 3.4, measures introduced over the past year—including the $29.5 billion debt swap in June, tax reforms in late June that resulted in an effective depreciation of the peso for non-energy trade, the zero deficit law approved in July, and the augmentation of Argentina's program with the IMF in August—failed to produce a sustained improvement in investor sentiment and reduction in interest rates spreads. Instead, the deteriorating economic outlook has heightened financial market concerns about the sustainability of current fiscal, exchange rate, and financing arrangements. Against this background, the

Box 3.3. The Effects of the September 11 Attacks on the Caribbean Region

The member countries of the Caribbean Community (CARICOM) are characterized mainly by small size and population, vulnerability to hurricanes, and high production costs in agriculture that stem from relatively high wages and low productivity.[1] Social indicators are generally favorable, although unemployment is high, with official rates ranging from 8 percent to 17 percent. Low productivity, and the impending reduction in preferential access for sugar and banana exports to the EU market, have contributed to a downturn in agriculture and increased reliance on tourism, which is the most important source of incomes and economic activity in most countries. The sector's contribution to economic activity ranges from about 7 percent in The Dominican Republic to near 50 percent in The Bahamas, and some estimates indicate that one in four jobs in the region depends on tourism. As a percentage of GDP, tourism earnings range from 15 percent in Belize and Dominica to more than 40 percent for Antigua and Barbuda and St. Lucia (see the figure).

The region's prospects, which already were being adversely affected by the slowdown in the U.S. economy by mid-2001, have worsened considerably following the September 11 attacks. The sharp drop in visitors after September 11 has led to a fall in economic activity and incomes, and increased unemployment and underemployment as some hotels have closed while others have reduced the length of the work week.[2] With a weakening of a significant proportion of the revenue base, fiscal and external positions have also begun to deteriorate. Preliminary estimates are that an external financing gap ranging from $1–2 billion (2 per-

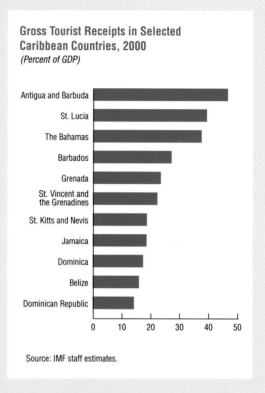

Gross Tourist Receipts in Selected Caribbean Countries, 2000
(Percent of GDP)

Source: IMF staff estimates.

cent to 4 percent of GDP) for the region as a whole could emerge in 2002.

The Region's Response

As the crisis developed, efforts were made to develop a prompt, coordinated regional response. In late September, member countries of the Eastern Caribbean Currency Union (ECCU)[3] agreed to:
- restrain the growth of public expenditure, and speed up public sector reforms aimed at greater efficiency;
- discontinue discretionary tax concessions that are widely used in the region to promote tourism and manufacturing; and

[1]Four countries, the Dominican Republic, Haiti, Jamaica, and Trinidad and Tobago, account for about 80 percent of the region's population. The average population of the other 11 countries is about 250,000. These latter countries are the six independent member countries of the ECCU (see footnote 3 below), and The Bahamas, Barbados, Belize, Guyana, Suriname.

[2]Hotel occupancy rates in some countries have fallen to about 15 percent or less, compared with an average for September-October of about 60 percent.

[3]The union comprises Anguilla and Montserrat, which are British territories, and Antigua and Barbuda, Dominica, Grenada, St. Kitts and Nevis, St. Lucia, and St. Vincent and the Grenadines. Monetary and exchange rate policies of the Union are administered by the Eastern Caribbean Central Bank (ECCB).

- convene meetings of labor, business, and government representatives to reach agreement on a framework for prices, wages, and employment.

Also, at the conclusion of an emergency meeting of the Caribbean Community (CARICOM) on October 12, the heads of government reached agreement on (1) approaching the IDB and the European Union (under the ACP-EU Convention), with proposals for emergency financing; (2) allocating additional budgetary resources for tourism promotion, mainly in the U.S., U.K., and Canadian markets; (3) strengthening airport security; and (4) implementing the recent UN Security Council resolution regarding the treatment of funds used to support terrorist activities. In addition, a number of governments in the region have begun approaching the Caribbean Development Bank, the Inter-American Development Bank, and the World Bank for financial assistance.

Governments in a number of countries have announced specific measures to address the deterioration of their economic situation. In many cases these measures comprise expenditure cuts, especially in low-priority capital projects, materials and supplies, government travel, some salaries, and overtime pay. Several countries have also announced freezes in civil service employment and a strengthening of revenue administration. In a few cases, governments have announced plans for a fiscal stimulus package, the relaxation of monetary policy, and borrowing from the international markets or the banking system. Other measures are likely to be announced in the context of the annual budget presentations for a number of countries that will be made in late 2001 and early 2002.

The Response of the IMF

The IMF, jointly with other institutions like the World Bank, the Caribbean Development Bank, and the ECCB, has focused its initial efforts on assessing the macroeconomic impact of the crisis, and working with countries to develop appropriate policy responses. These efforts will be supported by technical assistance from the IMF in fiscal and financial sector policies provided on an ongoing basis through the recently established Caribbean Center for Technical Assistance (CARTAC) that is based in Barbados. IMF staff have also begun to discuss possible financial support through the existing facilities, such as Stand-By Arrangements, and the Compensatory Financing Facility (CFF)—which is designed to provide assistance to cover shortfalls in export receipts (including from tourism) stemming from external shocks.

Argentine authorities have approached their creditors to negotiate a restructuring of debt. In tandem with appropriate macroeconomic policies, such an arrangement should be designed to restore fiscal solvency and lay the basis for a return to sustainable growth.

With indicators of production, spending, and confidence registering sharp declines in the third quarter, real GDP in Argentina is now expected to contract by 2¾ percent in 2001, including a fall of over 10 percent in investment spending, lower consumption, and a positive contribution to growth from net exports—largely because of declining imports. Consumer prices are expected to fall by 1 percent in the year as a whole, and producer prices by around 4 percent. Looking ahead, while the situation remains subject to great uncertainty, output is likely to fall in 2002, with deflation continuing (although at a slower rate than in 2001).

Contagion from the most recent financial turmoil in Argentina on other Latin American economies has generally been limited—in part because the latest round of difficulties was well anticipated by financial markets (see Chapter I, Appendix). In Brazil, interest rate spreads, equity markets, and the exchange rate deteriorated sharply immediately after the terrorist attacks in September but, thanks in part to continued strong policy implementation, these variables

Box 3.4. Argentina: An Uphill Struggle to Regain Confidence

After a decade of high growth, low inflation, and important progress in structural reform following the adoption of the convertibility regime in 1991, the performance of the Argentine economy deteriorated in 1999. This deterioration was partly the result of remaining domestic disequilibria, a weakening of policies, and a worsening of the external environment.

Argentina has continued to battle with a recession since then, reigniting doubts regarding the sustainability of the fiscal position and the exchange rate regime. In December 2000, the Argentine authorities put forward a revamped economic program that sought to bolster economic growth through a modest fiscal expansion and various structural measures, set in a framework that ensured medium-term fiscal sustainability. In support of the program, the IMF approved, in January 2001, an augmentation and front-loading of resources under the Stand-By Arrangement that was in place since March 2000.

In the event, the December 2000 program proved unsuccessful in restoring market confidence in Argentina's capacity to grow and maintain fiscal solvency within the framework of the convertibility regime. The authorities took advantage of the favorable market conditions of early 2001 to accelerate the borrowings contemplated in their financing plan; however, clear signs of fiscal strain began to emerge in mid-February after press reports showed that there had been sizable revenue shortfalls and spending overruns in December and January. On March 2, 2001, Economy Minister Jose Luis Machinea resigned amidst strong political resistance to adhere to the fiscal targets agreed with the IMF.

A broadly similar pattern was repeated on several other occasions during the year, notably following the announcement of Economy Minister Ricardo Lopez-Murphy's plan of across-the-board budget cuts in mid-March, of Minister Domingo Cavallo's late March plan of selective tax concessions and higher import tariffs, of the late-May "mega swap," of the mid-June plan that included further tax cuts and a mechanism to compensate non-energy exporters and importers for the strength of the U.S. dollar vis-à-vis the euro, and of the "zero-deficit" plan of July 11. Each time, the Argentine authorities reiterated their commitment to fiscal prudence, the timely service of government debt, and the convertibility regime, and proposed or adopted measures aimed at bolstering the confidence of domestic and foreign investors, and of the public in general. Although there were reservations about some of the measures, the authorities' resolve to maintain the convertibility regime was supported by the official community, including through the provision of additional financial resources in early September to help dispel concerns about a debt default.

None of these plans, however, proved to be sufficient to restore market confidence on a lasting basis. Following the announcement of the "zero-deficit" plan on July 11, *Moody's* and *Standard & Poor's* lowered by one notch their sovereign rating for Argentina, and the country's EMBI spread widened more than 300 basis points (see the figure). The downrating fueled a large withdrawal of bank deposits that put enormous pressure on domestic interest rates and on tax revenues. The withdrawal continued through late August, when the IMF announced its plans to augment Argentina's Stand-By credit by $8 billion. Other confidence indicators also deteriorated during this period: *Moody's* lowered Argentina's debt rating one more notch on July 26, the consumer confidence index fell sharply, tax revenues plummeted, and private growth forecasts for 2001 were revised downward well into negative territory.

Despite the official backing from Congress to the "zero-deficit plan," the clear resolve of Finance Minister Cavallo and President de la Rua, progress in reducing discretionary expenditures, and the additional resources provided by the IMF, a recovery in confidence continued to prove elusive following the completion of the fourth review of the Stand-By arrangement on September 7. Although some $2.5 billion of private sector deposits returned to the banking system and domestic interest rates fell markedly, most indicators of confidence for the months of September and October did not show any im-

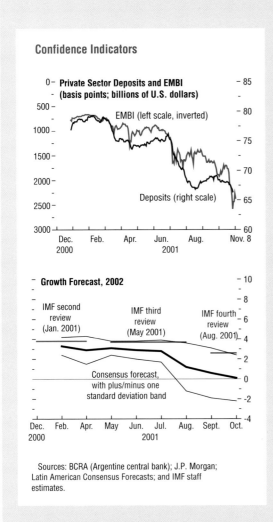

Confidence Indicators

Private Sector Deposits and EMBI
(basis points; billions of U.S. dollars)

EMBI (left scale, inverted)

Deposits (right scale)

Dec. Feb. Apr. Jun. Aug. Nov. 8
2000 2001

Growth Forecast, 2002

IMF second
review
(Jan. 2001)

IMF third
review
(May 2001)

IMF fourth
review
(Aug. 2001)

Consensus forecast,
with plus/minus one
standard deviation band

Dec. Feb. Apr. May Jun. Jul. Aug. Sept. Oct.
2000 2001

Sources: BCRA (Argentine central bank); J.P. Morgan;
Latin American Consensus Forecasts; and IMF staff
estimates.

provement, and some of them, like the EMBI
spread, continued to deteriorate, in part due to
global risk aversion following the September 11
attacks. Tax revenues also declined further, in
part reflecting declining growth and deteriorating domestic financial conditions. Days before
the congressional elections of October 14,
Standard & Poor's and *Moody's* downrated
Argentina's debt once again. The outcome of the
elections slowed agreement on the spending cuts
needed to comply with the zero-deficit plan in
the rest of 2001 and 2002, and on the reform of
the revenue-sharing agreement with the
provinces (although considerable progress was
made subsequently). Faced with these con-

straints, on October 29 the Argentine government announced that it would seek a voluntary
restructuring of all its bonded debt (about $100
billion), arguing that it was the only path left to
restore fiscal solvency and revive economic
growth. One week after the announcement, the
EMBI had shot up 500 basis points and *Standard
& Poor's* had placed Argentine debt on its "selective default" category; bank deposits, however, remained relatively stable.

In early November, the government announced that the restructuring of its bonded
debt would proceed in two phases. The first
phase, designed primarily for local bondholders
(banks, pension funds, mutual funds) comprised the exchange of eligible bonds for domestic loans of a lower yield backed by ear-
marked tax revenues. Over $50 billion of
government bonds (including from the
provinces) were swapped for those loans on
November 30. The government expects to complete the second phase of the restructuring
within the next three months.

The authorities placed a cap on deposit interest rates in late November equivalent to the
market average of 12 percent. A few days earlier,
a projected fiscal outturn for 2001 that ex-
ceeded by more than $1 billion the end-year tar-
get contained in the IMF program was announced. The combination dealt another blow
to confidence. During the last week of the
month, deposit outflows resumed, bank liquidity
dried up, interest rates skyrocketed, and the
EMBI spread reached an all-time high of more
than 3300 basis points. To arrest the outflow of
deposits and avoid the collapse of the financial
system, on December 1 the authorities introduced wide-ranging controls on banking and
foreign exchange transactions. These included
setting a monthly limit on withdrawals from individual bank accounts; prohibiting banks from
granting loans in pesos and from operating in
the peso market; putting a cap on interest rates
on peso deposits; and introducing foreign exchange restrictions on travel and transfers
abroad. The authorities stressed that all the
measures were transitory and aimed at safe-

Box 3.4 *(concluded)*

guarding the convertibility of bank deposits, and said that they would be revoked after 90 days, when the next phase of the debt restructuring is finalized.

Given the large uncertainty surrounding Argentina's prospects, economic projections—notably of GDP growth—are particularly problematic. Few doubt that output will fall, for a third year in a row in 2001. At the time of the

fourth review (in August), IMF staff projected a mild recovery in 2002 based on the pickup in confidence and bank credit that were to follow from the strict adherence to the zero deficit plan. The picture for 2002 is now much less clear, and the downside risks have increased. Correspondingly, the IMF staff and consensus forecast for 2002 growth in Argentina have been revised downward significantly (see Figure).

subsequently more than recovered their earlier losses, despite recent developments in Argentina. The continuing slowdown in the economy—with growth now projected to remain at around 2 percent in 2002—and the earlier depreciation of the *real* have begun to generate a sizable reduction in the external current account deficit, in turn helping to stabilize exchange rate expectations. Nevertheless, risks remain, both with respect to future developments in Argentina and uncertainties in the runup to next year's presidential election. Continued strong implementation of the policy program therefore remains crucial, including through the maintenance of tight fiscal and monetary policies and further progress with structural reform.

Elsewhere in Latin America, relatively high external financing requirements also remain the central vulnerability. These financing needs are typically linked to large public sector deficits and debt, a sizable share of which is linked to foreign currencies. Several countries are also exposed to commodity price risks—including Venezuela and Ecuador (oil), Chile (metals), and Colombia (coffee)—and to adverse developments in the region (Uruguay). While the potential risks vary substantially across countries, policies will need to be geared to maintaining investor confidence. These include a stronger adjustment effort in Venezuela, where the fiscal and external position will be hard hit by lower oil prices—although the oil stabilization fund will help to cushion these effects. Also needed are further progress

in banking and fiscal reforms in Ecuador and fiscal tightening and accelerated structural reforms in Uruguay.

The countries of Central and Eastern Europe and the Baltics also face substantial external financing requirements, given the persistently high current account deficits in most of these countries. International economic and financial market sentiment toward these countries appears to have remained generally strong, however, as indicated by robust inflows of direct investment and of other external funding. While these inflows could still be at risk if there is prolonged weakness in global activity, the favorable reaction to date may stem from the general improvements in economic fundamentals among these countries, including through privatization, other structural reforms, and, in most cases, generally sound macroeconomic policies.

As a result, the outlook for this region may in practice be more strongly influenced by its strong trade linkages with Western Europe (Figure 3.3). For example, export growth in the Czech Republic and Hungary is slowing from strong rates earlier this year, and a more generalized slowdown in trade appears likely as the impact of weaker activity in the European Union takes hold. But several factors appear to be contributing to a somewhat more robust outlook for this region than in the advanced economies, although with important divergences among individual countries. On the trade side, for example, the strong competitive position of these economies has enabled them to preserve and gain market share. In addition, structural changes—including recent and continuing inflows of foreign direct investment—have diversified the export base of many countries in this region and may have made exports less cyclically sensitive.

Domestic demand growth, supported in part by declining inflation across much of the region, should also help offset potential weaknesses in external trade. Reflecting this, growth of 3 to 3½ percent is expected in 2002 in much of central Europe, and of 4 to 4½ percent in southeastern Europe and the Baltics—only marginally weaker in many countries than in 2001. In Poland, by far the largest country in this region, the macroeconomic policy stance was tightened in 2001 to contain rising inflation pressures, and this contributed to relatively weak growth of 1½ percent this year. Monetary policy has been eased recently, however, and further relaxation is possible given the still high level of real interest rates. These steps are expected to help support a pickup in growth to around 2¼ percent in 2002.

Risks for the region as a whole appear tilted to the downside, however, especially in view of the general weakening of global growth. If activity should weaken sharply, there is only limited room for an easing of macroeconomic policies. As just noted, Poland—together with some other countries—has scope to ease monetary conditions, but inflation pressures remain of concern elsewhere (including in Hungary and Romania), and currency board arrangements in the Baltic countries and Bulgaria constrain their scope for independent monetary policy responses. The room for maneuver on fiscal policy is also quite limited, given rising deficits in some countries (Hungary and Poland, for example) and persistently high current account deficits in much of the region.

Economic prospects for Turkey—which had appeared to be improving from early August—have also been set back by the events of September 11 and their aftermath. While increases in interest rates and declines in prices immediately following the attacks have subsequently reversed, Turkey remains vulnerable to

Figure 3.3. Linkages Between Central and Western Europe[1]

There are close trade and growth linkages between central and western Europe, and foreign direct investment inflows to central Europe—much of this from the European Union—have been rising strongly.

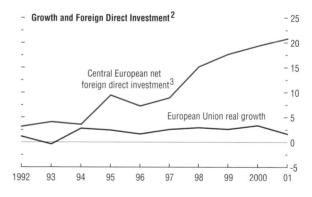

Sources: *Direction of Trade Statistics*, IMF; and IMF staff estimates.
[1] Includes Czech Republic, Hungary, Poland, Slovak Republic, and Slovenia.
[2] Foreign direct investment in U.S. dollars; European Union growth rate in percent.
[3] Includes Bulgaria, Czech Republic, Estonia, Hungary, Latvia, Lithuania, Poland, Romania, Slovak Republic, and Slovenia.

further downturns in investor sentiment given its high domestic and external financing requirements. These financing concerns have been heightened by the prospect of lower access to international financial markets, an unfavorable climate for privatization, and weaker growth in export earnings, including from tourism. With economic recovery further delayed, the economy is now projected to contract even more severely in 2001—with output falling by 6 percent—and to pick up more slowly in 2002—with growth reaching around 4 percent. The disinflation process has been hampered in 2001 by a further depreciation of the exchange rate, which has weakened by over 50 percent against the dollar since the beginning of the year; in 2002 inflation is expected to decline but to be substantially higher than projected in the previous *World Economic Outlook*. In light of this deterioration, the authorities have taken additional measures to ensure that the 2002 fiscal targets are met, and intend to formulate a strengthened adjustment program for 2002 to 2004. This program will build on the progress already made in macroeconomic and financial stabilization, and be accompanied by decisive steps to complete banking sector reform, revitalize privatization and private sector development, and improve public sector governance and efficiency.

Commodity Exporting Countries

The third broad-based influence on economic prospects for many emerging markets comes from developments in commodity prices. The sharp weakening of the outlook for global growth in the aftermath of September 11 has led to a significant decline in oil prices and further falls in prices of most nonfuel commodities. The impact of lower commodity prices will vary significantly, depending on the structure of the economy and the previous stance of policies. In general, oil exporters are likely to be most severely affected, although in a number of countries—particularly in the Middle East—the impact will be cushioned as a result of the relatively conservative policies followed when prices were

high. Among nonfuel commodity exporters, the adverse impact will be offset in part by lower oil prices, so that growth for the group as a whole is relatively well sustained. The impact on poverty may be more marked, however, with lower prices for agricultural goods having a particularly strong effect on the poor in rural areas.

Looking first at the oil exporting countries—particularly in the Middle East, Africa, and the Commonwealth of Independent States (CIS)—lower production and prices of oil have contributed to a general weakening of projected growth for 2001 and 2002 compared with the exceptionally strong performance experienced in most of these countries in 2000 (Figure 3.4). With the oil market weakening further since the events of September 11, the 2001–02 growth projections for a number of these countries have been marked down compared with those in the October 2001 *World Economic Outlook*; in other cases, though, new data or country-specific developments have led to upward revisions to the outlook.

In the Middle East, the outlook for Saudi Arabia and Kuwait has weakened further in the light of recent oil market developments, with Saudi Arabia expected to grow by just over 1½ percent in 2002 compared with 4½ percent in 2000. Growth in the Islamic Republic of Iran is expected to continue at a relatively firm pace of around 5 percent, however, supported in part by continued recovery in agriculture and strong performance in the construction and manufacturing sectors. The outlook for the Middle East, particularly for non-oil producing countries, is influenced by a range of other pressures. These include increased regional security concerns, which have contributed to a downturn in tourism (of particular importance for Egypt, Israel, and Jordan); continuing weakness in the information technology sector (affecting Israel); and fiscal and external financing difficulties, possibly aggravated by a downturn in remittances from overseas (key risks in Lebanon).

In the CIS, activity in Russia and Kazakhstan is expected to slow somewhat from the strong pace of 2000 and 2001, although it should remain reasonably healthy, with growth of 3½ percent still expected in Russia in 2002 and 7 percent in Kazakhstan. In Russia, the climate for foreign investment appears to have improved, investment spending—particularly on energy-related projects—has been even stronger than earlier expected, and consumer spending has also been strong. While Russia remains vulnerable to lower oil prices, the impact is expected to be manageable unless the decline proves to be significantly deeper and more prolonged than currently anticipated. With growth estimates for 2001 now revised up substantially, the carryover effects of these changes have supported the 2002 outlook as well. The strength of activity in Russia is also contributing to reasonably firm growth among non-oil producing countries in the CIS—especially among countries that are more advanced in the transition process, such as Ukraine.

Among African oil-producing countries, the 2002 outlook for Algeria and Nigeria has been revised down compared with the October *World Economic Outlook*. In Algeria, the oil stabilization fund built up during the recent period of high oil prices will help cushion the downturn, and growth is expected to be relatively well sustained at around 3½ percent. Weaker growth of under 2 percent is expected in Nigeria, where the economy continues to be dominated by oil and where an effective stabilization mechanism to smooth the effects of oil price fluctuations has not been put in place. Angola is expected to grow by around 11 percent in 2002, supported by a sizable increase in oil production from new offshore fields.

Not surprisingly, the reduction in oil prices has led to a general weakening of current account positions among oil exporters (Figure 3.4). While surpluses are still expected in Russia, Algeria, and Venezuela in 2002—albeit much reduced from their recent levels and from earlier projections for 2002—lower oil prices have led to the emergence of external deficits in Saudi Arabia and Kazakhstan rather than previously projected surpluses. Of much more concern is Nigeria, where the current account deficit is now expected to reach over 10 percent of GDP in

Figure 3.4. Fuel and Nonfuel Commodity Exporting Countries

The outlook for growth, current account positions, and exports has weakened among fuel exporting countries since September. For nonfuel exporters, growth is projected to pick up in 2002, but to be lower than expected earlier.

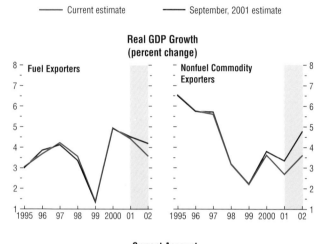

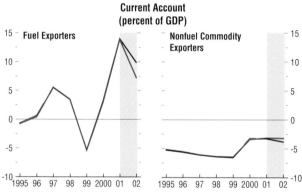

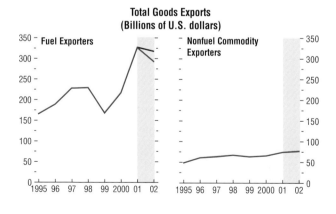

2002—more than double what is expected in 2001 and what was projected earlier for 2002.

Turning to nonfuel commodities, the further weakening in global economic activity and prospects since September 11 has pushed down the prices of most metals and agricultural commodities—many of which, including coffee, cotton, and copper, were already at depressed levels. These trends have weakened the outlook for many of the poorest countries—mainly in Africa—whose overall economic prospects are often closely tied to export earnings from a small range of nonfuel commodities. At the same time, however, lower oil prices are helping to offset the terms of trade deterioration among energy-importing countries and limiting the increase in their external financing requirements. In particular, while recent commodity price shocks imply additional terms of trade losses equivalent to around 5 to 10 percent of GDP in most of the main oil exporting countries, the impact on nonfuel exporters is much lower—generally in the range of –1 to 1 percent of GDP (see Chapter II).[5]

Reflecting these developments, growth of 3½ percent is projected for the oil importing countries of Africa in 2002, nearly 1 percentage point lower than in the October *World Economic Outlook*, but up from growth of 3¼ percent expected in 2001.[6] These countries' current account deficits are expected to deteriorate modestly to just under 3 percent of GDP, compared with 2.4 percent in 2001. Prospects for individual countries in this group vary widely, however, reflecting not only their particular mix of commodity trade but also economic policy developments and other country-specific influences. In South Africa, growth is expected to remain at around 2¼ percent, with inflation coming down and the current account in surplus. While the rand has weakened further as a result of regional and domestic factors, the country's vulnerability to external shocks has generally diminished—reflecting strong macroeconomic fundamentals, continuing reductions in the central bank's net open forward position (now at its lowest level in over a decade), and a healthy banking system. Elsewhere, relatively healthy growth in the range of 4 to 6 percent is expected in Cameroon, Ghana, Tanzania, and Uganda, and around 8 percent in Mozambique—countries where macroeconomic and structural policies have generally been sound. In contrast, weaker growth is expected to persist in Kenya, where policy implementation has been mixed; and the ongoing turmoil in Zimbabwe continues to undermine economic activity, with GDP expected to contract by around 6 percent in 2002.

Appendix: Alternative Scenario— Impact of a More Gradual Increase in Confidence and Risk Appetite

The baseline projections envisage that the global economy will start to recover during next year, based in part on an expected rebound in confidence and risk appetite over the course of 2002. However, the world economic outlook is still subject to considerable uncertainty, reflecting both the effects of the September 11 attacks and existing financial imbalances. In particular, policymakers need to consider the outcome if the synchronized slowing in output continues through 2002, reflecting a slower-than-anticipated rebound in consumer and business confidence and a more prolonged period of difficult financial market conditions for emerging market economies.

To illustrate some of the downside risks attached to the baseline projections, the alternative scenario assesses the implications if consumer and business confidence and risk appetite do not recover during 2002, using the IMF's multicountry macroeconometric model,

---

[5]Specifically, these are the terms of trade gains or losses arising under the commodity price baseline used in this interim *World Economic Outlook* relative to those arising in the baseline used in the October 2001 *World Economic Outlook*.

[6]As noted in the October *World Economic Outlook*, however, the IMF's projections for Africa have tended to be too optimistic, with outturns often lower than expected as a result of adverse shocks, including conflict, and shortfalls in policy implementation (see also Box 3.1).

MULTIMOD. In addition, results are reported for a separate block that is currently under development for emerging market economies.[7] The key assumptions underlying the scenario are that:

- *The lack of recovery in confidence* is modeled as a reduction in the propensity to consume relative to baseline that sum to around half of the estimated total impact on GDP if confidence were to remain depressed (see Chapter II), while the other half of the impact is already contained in the baseline scenario as confidence and financing conditions recover only gradually over 2002. In the United States, the marginal propensity to consume is assumed to drop relative to baseline by 1 percent in 2002 and by ½ percent in 2003, before reverting to baseline in 2004. In other industrial countries, the downward corrections to consumption are assumed to be half this size.

- The more gradual increase in global risk appetite is assumed to reduce equity prices in industrial countries by raising the discount rate on future profits as well as prolong the period during which emerging market economies face elevated risk premia and a curtailment of capital flows relative to the baselines. As a result, the discount rate is assumed to rise by ½ percentage point in the United States and ¼ percentage point elsewhere in 2002, then taper off. In emerging markets the risk premium is assumed to increase by 1 percentage point in 2002 compared to the baseline, equal to about half of the current impact, as measured by the widening in the EMBI+ spread between September 11 and early November. The risk premium is assumed to be ½ percent above baseline in 2003, before reverting to baseline in 2004.

In the alternative scenario, oil prices are assumed to fall in line with weakening demand. In addition, monetary authorities in both industrial countries and emerging economies are assumed to follow a forward-looking Taylor rule, responding to changes in expected inflation and the current output gap, so that nominal interest rates fall in response to the adverse shocks described above. In Japan, where nominal interest rates are close to their floor, some quantitative easing is also assumed. Finally, fiscal authorities allow automatic stabilizers to operate, but are not assumed to initiate discretionary policies.

The slower reversion of consumer and investor confidence is estimated to reduce global output relative to baseline by about ¾ percent in 2002 and about ¼ percent in 2003 (Table 3.5). In industrial countries, the fall in output is almost 1 percent in 2002, with the distribution across countries and regions depending on the size of the shock and on the room for maneuver on monetary policy. In particular, in Japan, where nominal interest rates are at their floor, deflation accelerates and increases real interest rates by more than ¾ percentage points relative to baseline in 2002, leading to an appreciation of Japan's real effective exchange rate (Figure 3.5). Altogether, the loss in output in 2002 relative to baseline due to the slower rebound in confidence is about 1 percent in the United States, ½ to ¾ percent in the euro area and other industrial country regions, and almost 1½ percent in Japan, even though the initial shock to Japan's domestic demand was assumed to be only half of that in the United States. The impact of weaker domestic demand in industrial countries and tighter foreign financing constraints would reduce output in developing countries as a whole by ¼ percent relative to baseline in 2002 and domestic demand by over 1 percent.

The failure of global risk appetite to recover and the fall in external demand from industrial countries is likely to have a particularly significant impact on emerging market economies.

---

[7]The emerging market block uses the results from the MULTIMOD simulation to provide the global environment. The feedback from the new block to the MULTIMOD simulation, however, is limited to the impact on capital flows to developing countries.

Table 3.5. Alternative Scenario: Delayed Strengthening in Consumer Confidence and Risk Appetite
(Percent deviation from baseline unless otherwise specified)

	2002	2003	2004	2005	2006
World real GDP	−0.7	−0.2	0.3	0.2	0.1
United States					
Real GDP	−0.9	−0.2	0.5	0.3	0.2
Domestic demand	−0.9	−0.2	0.5	0.3	0.2
Real effective exchange rate	−2.4	−1.2	−0.1	. . .	0.1
Current account ($billion)	1.0	36.9	38.9	17.2	11.5
CPI Inflation (percentage points)	−0.7	−0.7	−0.2	0.1	0.1
Short-term interest rate (percentage points)	−1.8	−1.2	−0.3	−0.1	−0.1
Short-term real interest rate (percentage points)	−1.2	−0.8	−0.2	−0.2	−0.2
Euro area					
Real GDP	−0.6	0.1	0.5	0.2	0.1
Domestic demand	−0.1	0.3	0.4	0.2	0.1
Real effective exchange rate	0.5	0.4	0.1	. . .	. . .
Real U.S. dollar exchange rate	2.3	1.2	0.1	−0.1	−0.1
Current account ($billion)	−7.6	−6.7	3.6	−3.4	−4.3
CPI inflation (percentage points)	−0.9	−0.7	−0.1	0.3	0.2
Short-term interest rate (percentage points)	−1.4	−0.8	−0.0	0.1	0.1
Short-term real interest rate (percentage points)	−0.8	−0.5	−0.1	−0.1	−0.1
Japan					
Real GDP	−1.4	−0.7	0.2	. . .	. . .
Domestic demand	−1.1	−0.5	−0.1	. . .	. . .
Real effective exchange rate	3.5	1.4	0.4	0.3	0.1
Real U.S. dollar exchange rate	4.5	1.9	0.4	0.2	. . .
Current account ($billion)	5.4	−10.9	−8.3	−7.2	−5.4
CPI inflation (percentage points)	−0.8	−0.6	−0.2	. . .	. . .
Short-term interest rate (percentage points)	. . .	−0.1	−0.2	0.1.	0.2
Short-term real interest rate (percentage points)	0.8	0.3	. . .	0.1	0.2
Other industrial economies					
Real GDP	−0.7	. . .	0.4	0.2	0.2
Real domestic demand	−0.2	0.2	0.3	0.2	0.1
Current account ($billion)	−21.2	−20.3	−5.6	−3.1	−3.4
Industrial countries					
Real GDP	−0.9	−0.2	0.4	0.2	0.1
Real domestic demand	−0.6	. . .	0.4	0.2	0.1
Current account ($billion)	−22.4	−1.1	28.6	3.5	−1.5
Developing countries					
Real GDP	−0.3	−0.1	0.1	0.1	0.1
Real domestic demand	−1.2	−0.6	0.3	0.1	0.1
Current account ($billion)	22.4	1.1	−28.6	−3.5	1.5
Memorandum					
Price of oil	−14.9	−16.2	−9.2	−1.5	−1.4

This issue is examined in more detail in Table 3.6, which is based on a new block for emerging market economies currently under development, and can be thought of as a model for emerging Latin American and Asian economies, with the important exceptions of China and India.[8] The higher risk premium reduces capital inflows to these countries by about $23 billion in 2002 and causes the exchange rate to depreciate. The rise in real interest rates, increase in the value of foreign currency denominated debt, and decline in the stock prices of domestic firms reduce wealth relative to the baseline, which in turn reduces private consumption and investment. However, the impact of the contraction in domestic demand on output is partially offset by

[8]The group comprises about one-third of developing countries' GDP.

an increase in the external balance as imports are reduced and exports boosted. Altogether, the delayed fall in the risk premium would reduce output in emerging market economies by almost 2 percent relative to baseline in 2002 and domestic demand by around 3½ percent (Figure 3.5).[9] Such an outcome would reduce global output compared to that reported in the earlier MULTIMOD scenario.

Given the large uncertainties surrounding the alternative scenario, it may be useful to provide ready reckoners of the individual shocks that comprise the overall scenario, so that the likely impact of alternative assumptions can be constructed. Table 3.7 provides such a breakdown for the three main components of the alternative scenario: lower consumer confidence, higher risk aversion, and a fall in the oil price (the endogenous impact of lower oil prices has been eliminated from the other two ready reckoner calculations). The fall in consumer confidence relative to baseline has a substantial impact on output in 2002, particularly in the United States and Japan, which is then largely reversed in 2003—hence this is best thought of as a large temporary disturbance focused on the industrial countries. By contrast, higher risk aversion has a smaller but more persistent impact in most industrial countries, with the important exception of Japan. The simulation using the emerging market economies block also indicates that it could also have a substantial impact on parts of Asia and Latin America that are relatively open to trade and capital flows. Finally, lower oil prices provide mild support for global activity. Indeed, the effect could be somewhat larger than the simulation indicates, as MULTIMOD does not capture the impact of changes in prices of other energy products, such as gas, which tend to follow the price of oil.

These scenarios should be regarded as illustrative of the potential downside risks facing the

[9]In addition, a change in the risk premium could also have supply-side, credit rationing effects if banks experience a large increase in nonperforming foreign loans.

Figure 3.5. Impact of a Delayed Reversion in Global Confidence and Risk Appetite

If global confidence and risk appetite reverse more slowly than assumed in the baseline, real domestic demand and growth will also be lower than expected in all major economies.

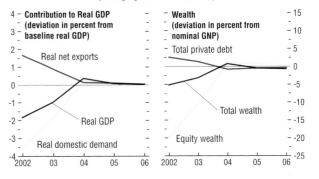

Source: IMF staff estimates.

Table 3.6. Alternative Scenario: Delayed Recovery in Financing Flows to Emerging Markets
(Percent deviation from baseline unless otherwise specified)

	2002	2003	2004	2005	2006
Emerging Market Borrowers					
Real GDP	−1.8	−0.9	0.4	0.1	0.1
Domestic demand	−3.4	−1.8	0.3	. . .	. . .
Real exports	1.4	0.7	0.1	. . .	. . .
Real imports	−3.8	−1.9	−0.2	−0.2	−0.1
Nominal effective exchange rate	−4.7	−2.4	−0.3	0.1	0.2
Real competitiveness index	−2.7	−1.3	−0.2	. . .	. . .
Current account ($billion)	22.9	14.0	0.9	3.9	2.7
Total wealth	−2.2	−1.2	0.5	0.1	. . .
Market value of capital stock	−8.4	−4.4	0.4	0.2	0.1
Real capital stock	−0.3	−0.1	−0.3	−0.2	−0.2
Domestic private debt (percentage points of GNP)	0.3	0.2	−0.7	−0.4	−0.3
Foreign private debt (percentage points of GNP)	2.1	1.1	−0.2	−0.2	−0.2
CPI inflation (percentage points)	0.6	0.3	−0.1	−0.1	−0.1
Short-term interest rate (percentage points)	0.6	0.3	−0.4	−0.1	. . .
Short-term real interest rate (percentage points)	0.5	0.3	−0.5	−0.1	. . .
Yields on domestic private debt (percentage points)	2.3	1.1	−0.3	−0.1	−0.1
Yields on foreign private debt (percentage points)	1.2	0.6	. . .	. . .	. . .

Table 3.7. Ready Reckoners of Individual Shock[1]
(Percent deviation from baseline)

	Real GDP					
	Higher risk aversion lower confidence reduces U.S. consumption by 1 percent and ½ percent elsewhere[2]		Reduces U.S. investment by ½ percent and ¼ percent elsewhere[3]		Oil prices lower by 10 percent in 2002 and by 5 percent in 2003	
	2002	2003	2002	2003	2002	2003
Global economy	−0.4	−0.1	−0.3	−0.2	. . .	0.1
Industrial countries	−0.5	−0.2	−0.3	−0.2	. . .	0.1
United States	−0.6	−0.2	−0.3	−0.2	0.1	0.1
Euro area	−0.3	−0.1	−0.2	−0.1	0.1	0.1
Japan	−0.6	−0.3	−0.7	−0.3	. . .	. . .
Developing countries	−0.1	. . .	−0.1	−0.1	. . .	0.1
Memorandum						
Emerging markets	−0.1	. . .	−1.8	−0.9	0.1	0.1

[1]These results are generated using a version of MULTIMOD that contains a linear relationship between inflation and demand conditions.

[2]In the United States, lower confidence is assumed to reduce the marginal propensity to consume by 1 percent in 2002 and by ½ percent in 2003, before reverting to baseline in 2004. In the other industrial countries, the negative shock to consumption is assumed to be half this size. Developing and emerging economies are not assumed to suffer any direct shock to domestic consumption.

[3]In the United States, the flight to quality is assumed to increase the risk premium on equities in the United States by ½ percent in 2002 and by ¼ percent in 2003, before reverting to baseline in 2004. In the other industrial countries, the increase in the risk premium is assumed to be half this size. Developing economies are not assumed to suffer any direct shock to risk aversion. Emerging markets face a rise in default risk by 1 percent in 2002 and by ½ percent in 2003.

world economy if the recent deterioration in confidence and increase in global risk aversion are maintained through 2002. The implication is that global growth could fall below 2 percent in 2002, similar to levels experienced in 1975, 1981, and 1991.

References

Loungani, Prakash, 2000, "How Accurate Are Private Sector Forecasts—Cross-Country Evidence from Consensus Forecasts of Output Growth," IMF Working Paper No. 00/77 (Washington: International Monetary Fund).

SUMMING UP BY THE ACTING CHAIR

The following remarks by the Acting Chair summarize the Executive Board's discussion of the Interim World Economic Outlook, *which took place on December 11, 2001.*

Directors observed that at the time of the October 2001 *World Economic Outlook* update, the global economic outlook in the near term was being affected by a sharp slowdown in growth in almost all major regions of the world, accompanied by a marked decline in trade growth, significantly lower commodity prices, and deteriorating financing conditions in emerging markets. Nevertheless, in the immediate period prior to the terrorist attacks of September 11, there appeared to be a reasonable prospect of recovery in late 2001. However, more recent data, on which the interim *World Economic Outlook* revisions are based, indicate that the situation before the attacks was in fact weaker than earlier projected in many regions, including the United States, Europe, and Japan. Directors accordingly concluded that the tragic events of September 11 had exacerbated an already very difficult situation in the global economy.

Impact of September 11

Directors observed that, in the aftermath of the September 11 attacks, consumer and business confidence weakened further across the globe. There was a significant initial impact on demand and activity, particularly in the United States, although there are signs that this is now beginning to stabilize. Turning to financial markets, Directors observed that there had been an initial generalized shift away from risky assets in both mature and emerging markets, including a substantial deterioration in financing conditions for emerging market economies. Between end-September and early December 2001, however,

financial markets generally strengthened, as equity markets recovered and the earlier flight to quality began to reverse. A few Directors cautioned that this recovery in financial markets may reflect an overreaction following the attacks and the subsequent monetary response, and should not be seen as indicating that a recovery is in sight. Movements in major exchange rates on net have been moderate, while commodity prices have fallen back further, especially for oil, as the outlook for global growth has weakened.

Directors expressed particular concern about the synchronicity of the slowdown across nearly all regions, reflected, among other things, in the recent data on employment declines and the softening in labor markets. They noted that, to a considerable extent, this synchronicity is the result of common shocks, including the initial increase in oil prices and the bursting of the information technology bubble. Increased international linkages, particularly in the financial and corporate sectors, have also played a role.

Directors noted that the more pronounced economic slowdown and worsening financing conditions have adversely affected many emerging markets through trade and confidence channels, constraining capital flows, including foreign direct investment. Countries with substantial external financing requirements remain vulnerable to potential reassessments of global and domestic economic prospects and to further shocks to international capital markets. Nevertheless, Directors considered that recently most emerging markets have become more resilient to external shocks as a result of improved macroeconomic management, broad-based structural reforms, and flexible exchange rates. They also noted signs of increased investors' discrimination across countries, which was helping to limit contagion risks.

Directors observed that developing countries and, in particular, the poorest countries are being hurt by weaker external demand and falling commodity prices, with oil exporters particularly affected. Nonfuel commodity exporters will also be affected by further weakness in already depressed prices, although for some the benefits from lower oil prices will limit the increase in external financing requirements. Thus, while growth is projected to be relatively well sustained for the group as a whole, the outlook for individual countries varies widely. Directors were also concerned that this overall outlook may mask the true impact on poverty, as lower prices for agricultural goods will hurt rural areas, while the benefits of lower oil prices tend to accrue in relatively more prosperous urban areas.

Outlook for 2002

Directors considered that the current outlook remains subject to considerable uncertainty, reflecting in part the inherent unpredictability of changes in confidence and financial market sentiment, and evidenced for example by the sharp increase in dispersion in private sector forecasts. Notwithstanding these uncertainties, they observed that a number of factors should help to support recovery in 2002. *First,* policymakers have generally moved quickly to support activity, and, with much of the resulting stimulus still in the pipeline, significant support will be provided to activity in the course of 2002. *Second,* oil prices have weakened sharply as a result of weakening demand, which could provide support for global activity, although there are clearly negative effects for oil producers, including a number of highly indebted countries. *Third,* the completion of ongoing inventory corrections will provide support to demand. *Finally,* the strengthening of economic fundamentals in many countries in recent years—notably lower inflation, generally improved fiscal positions, stronger external finan-

cial positions in many emerging market economies, especially in Asia, and the shift toward more flexible exchange rates—has increased the room for policy maneuver and resilience to external shocks.

Risks to Recovery

Directors acknowledged that the above factors may support the possibility that recovery in 2002 could come more rapidly than presently expected, particularly if the policy stimulus in the pipeline produces a faster or stronger impact and if confidence revives more sharply than assumed. Nevertheless, Directors believed that the possibility of a worse outcome still remains the major global policy concern, and identified three interlinked areas of risk. *First,* confidence and activity *in the United States* may pick up more slowly than currently expected, possibly as a result of the imbalances accumulated in the past. There are also downside risks to activity in the other major currency areas. These could reinforce the already synchronized downturn, with negative consequences for developing countries through a reduced desire for risk taking in financial markets and lower commodity prices. *Second,* the outlook for many emerging market economies will continue to depend on developments in global risk aversion; while recent developments have been encouraging, market access for many countries remains limited. *Third,* many Directors noted that the imbalances in the global economy remain an important source of risk. All Directors agreed that, against this background, the economic situation merits continued close monitoring.

Policy Challenges Ahead

Directors believed that the primary challenge faced by policymakers is how best to support the prospects for recovery and to limit the risks attendant on a deeper and longer downturn. Given the synchronicity of the slowdown, policies in both advanced and developing countries must be viewed in a global perspective to ensure that there is adequate global demand. *Monetary policy*—the most flexible instrument—has appropriately played the primary role to date, and most Directors agreed that there remains room for further easing if weakness persists, including through a more aggressive approach to monetary easing in Japan.

Turning to fiscal policy, given the limitations of monetary policy in the current environment of weak confidence and excess capacity, most Directors agreed that *fiscal policy* should also play a role, particularly through the operation of the automatic stabilizers, although the room for maneuver will depend on each country's medium-term consolidation objectives. Additional stimulus presently under consideration *in the United States* could be helpful if implemented sufficiently rapidly while demand is still weak, and should be carefully designed to shore up consumer confidence and boost activity in the short run, without exacerbating medium-term fiscal pressures. *In Europe,* some Directors thought that the automatic stabilizers should be allowed to operate in full, and a few Directors saw room for well-designed moderate discretionary policies in some countries in the region. *In Japan,* the recent supplementary budget has gone a significant way toward avoiding a withdrawal of stimulus in the current recessionary environment. Structural reforms in Europe and, particularly, in Japan, remain crucial, both to improve growth potential and boost confidence, and to help reduce global imbalances over the longer term.

In developing and emerging markets, there is generally considerably less room for policy maneuver to support growth, although where it exists it should be used. In particular, Directors were of the view that, in the difficult external environment, many emerging market economies have little alternative but to implement even much deeper reforms to strengthen (or even restore)

their economic fundamentals, and ensure future access to finance at acceptable spreads so as to sustain growth. More generally, domestic policies should be geared to achieving early external adjustment where necessary, accompanied by structural reforms—particularly of the financial and corporate sectors—to help reduce vulnerability.

For its part, the international community should provide strong support for such efforts, through the international financial institutions and other channels, and due attention will need to be paid to the appropriate mix between adjustment and financing. For the poorest countries, additional concessional financing may be required. A few Directors reiterated the call for improved market access to industrial country markets, as well as for a rapid increase in official development assistance toward the U.N. target of 0.7 percent of GNP.

Finally, there remains an important question as to the potential long-term impact of increased security concerns and other related issues, including transportation costs on economic activity. While it is impossible to estimate their size with any precision at this stage, and there will be a short-term impact on productivity, Directors noted that such costs are likely to be concentrated in a few industries, and, at this stage, it is not anticipated that they will be large enough or long lasting to have a significant impact on medium- and long-term growth trends, although a few Directors considered that more widespread effects remain possible. Nonetheless, this reinforces the need to press forward with structural and other reforms designed to increase long-run productive potential. Directors underlined, in this connection, that the agreement reached at the World Trade Organization meetings in Doha in November to launch new trade negotiations is of particular importance, as they can be expected to contribute substantially to global economic growth over the medium term.

STATISTICAL APPENDIX

Eight statistical tables are included in this appendix. They focus on global developments and represent a subset of the traditional 46 Statistical Appendix tables in the *World Economic Outlook*. Data in these tables have been compiled on the basis of information available through early December 2001.

Assumptions

Key assumptions underlying the estimates for 2001 and beyond are:

- Real effective *exchange rates* for the advanced economies are assumed to remain constant at their average levels during the period September 17–October 16, 2001, except for the currencies participating in the European exchange rate mechanism II (ERM II), which are assumed to remain constant in nominal terms relative to the euro. These assumptions imply an average U.S. dollars/SDR conversion rate of 1.277 in 2001 and 1.285 in 2002.
- Established *policies* of national authorities are assumed to be maintained.
- It is assumed that the *price of oil* will average $24.25 a barrel in 2001 and $18.50 a barrel in 2002; thereafter, the oil price assumption is based on market information on long-term futures and swaps.
- With regard to *interest rates*, it is assumed that the London interbank offered rate (LIBOR) on six-month U.S. dollar deposits will average 3.8 percent in 2001 and 2.8 percent in 2002.

For a full description of *World Economic Outlook* data and conventions, as well as the classification of countries in the various groups presented in the following tables, see the October 2001 *World Economic Outlook*, pp. 181–92.

List of Tables

Table 1. World Output[1]

(Annual percent change)

	Average 1983–92	1993	1994	1995	1996	1997	1998	1999	2000	2001	2002
World	**3.5**	**2.3**	**3.7**	**3.6**	**4.0**	**4.2**	**2.8**	**3.6**	**4.7**	**2.4**	**2.4**
Advanced economies	**3.3**	**1.4**	**3.4**	**2.7**	**3.0**	**3.4**	**2.7**	**3.3**	**3.9**	**1.1**	**0.8**
Major advanced economies	3.2	1.3	3.1	2.3	2.8	3.2	2.8	3.0	3.5	1.0	0.6
United States	3.4	2.7	4.0	2.7	3.6	4.4	4.3	4.1	4.1	1.0	0.7
Japan	3.9	0.5	1.0	1.4	3.6	1.8	−1.0	0.7	2.2	−0.4	−1.0
Germany	3.1	−1.1	2.3	1.7	0.8	1.4	2.0	1.8	3.0	0.5	0.7
France	2.2	−0.9	1.8	1.9	1.1	1.9	3.5	3.0	3.5	2.1	1.3
Italy	2.3	−0.9	2.2	2.9	1.1	2.0	1.8	1.6	2.9	1.8	1.2
United Kingdom	2.5	2.5	4.7	2.9	2.6	3.4	3.0	2.1	2.9	2.3	1.8
Canada	2.6	2.4	4.7	2.8	1.6	4.3	3.9	5.1	4.4	1.4	0.8
Other advanced economies	3.9	1.9	4.6	4.3	3.8	4.3	2.2	4.9	5.2	1.5	1.9
Memorandum											
European Union	2.6	−0.3	2.8	2.5	1.7	2.6	2.9	2.6	3.4	1.7	1.3
Euro area	2.7	−0.8	2.3	2.3	1.4	2.3	2.9	2.6	3.4	1.5	1.2
Newly industrialized Asian economies	8.2	6.5	7.7	7.5	6.3	5.8	−2.4	7.9	8.2	0.4	2.0
Developing countries	**4.7**	**6.4**	**6.7**	**6.1**	**6.5**	**5.8**	**3.6**	**3.9**	**5.8**	**4.0**	**4.4**
Regional groups											
Africa	2.0	0.4	2.3	3.0	5.5	3.1	3.5	2.5	2.8	3.5	3.5
Developing Asia	7.3	9.4	9.7	9.0	8.3	6.5	4.0	6.2	6.8	5.6	5.6
Middle East, Malta, and Turkey	3.5	3.5	0.3	4.2	5.1	5.1	4.1	1.1	5.9	1.8	3.9
Western Hemisphere	2.3	4.0	5.0	1.8	3.6	5.3	2.3	0.1	4.1	1.0	1.7
Analytical groups											
By source of export earnings											
Fuel	2.6	0.6	0.1	3.1	3.7	4.2	3.6	1.4	4.9	4.4	3.6
Nonfuel	5.0	7.1	7.4	6.5	6.8	5.9	3.6	4.2	5.8	3.9	4.5
By external financing source											
Net debtor countries	4.8	6.5	6.9	6.3	6.6	5.9	3.6	4.0	5.8	4.0	4.5
of which, official financing	2.6	1.6	2.4	5.4	5.3	4.2	3.9	3.7	3.8	4.2	4.0
Net debtor countries by debt-servicing experience											
Countries with arrears and/or rescheduling during 1994–98	2.7	3.6	4.6	5.2	5.0	4.4	−0.4	2.0	4.5	3.2	3.4
Countries in transition	**0.2**	**−8.9**	**−8.6**	**−1.4**	**−0.6**	**1.6**	**−0.8**	**3.6**	**6.3**	**4.9**	**3.6**
Central and eastern Europe	...	−0.3	3.0	5.6	3.9	2.6	2.3	2.0	3.8	3.0	3.2
CIS and Mongolia	...	−12.6	−14.6	−5.5	−3.3	1.1	−2.8	4.6	7.8	6.1	3.9
Russia	...	−13.0	−13.5	−4.2	−3.4	0.9	−4.9	5.4	8.3	5.8	3.6
Excluding Russia	...	−11.8	−17.0	−8.6	−3.1	1.5	1.6	2.8	6.8	6.8	4.6
Memorandum											
Median growth rate											
Advanced economies	3.2	0.7	4.1	2.9	3.0	3.7	3.4	3.7	3.8	1.6	1.3
Developing countries	3.4	3.1	3.8	4.3	4.6	4.4	3.7	3.5	3.9	3.3	3.2
Countries in transition	...	−8.1	−3.0	2.1	3.0	3.7	3.8	3.3	5.1	4.5	4.1
Output per capita											
Advanced economies	2.9	0.8	2.7	2.1	2.3	2.8	2.1	2.8	2.5	0.5	0.3
Developing countries	2.4	4.4	4.9	4.5	4.8	4.2	1.9	2.3	4.3	2.5	3.0
Countries in transition	...	−9.0	−8.6	−1.4	−0.3	2.0	−0.5	4.1	6.1	5.2	4.0
World growth based on market exchange rates	**3.1**	**1.1**	**2.9**	**2.8**	**3.2**	**3.5**	**2.3**	**3.0**	**4.0**	**1.4**	**1.2**
Value of world output in billions of U.S. dollars											
At market exchange rates	23,863	24,442	26,234	29,095	29,818	29,680	29,487	30,550	31,362	31,117	31,920
At purchasing power parities	22,806	30,467	32,170	33,996	36,032	38,227	39,652	41,585	44,549	47,473	50,612

[1]Real GDP.

Table 2. Employment and Unemployment in Advanced Economies
(Percent)

	Average[1] 1983–92	1993	1994	1995	1996	1997	1998	1999	2000	2001	2002
Growth in employment											
Advanced economies	**1.3**	**−0.1**	**1.1**	**1.2**	**1.0**	**1.5**	**1.0**	**1.3**	**1.4**	**0.4**	**0.2**
Major advanced economies	1.2	–	1.0	0.8	0.8	1.4	1.0	1.1	1.2	0.1	−0.1
United States	1.8	1.5	2.3	1.5	1.5	2.3	1.5	1.5	1.3	−0.2	0.2
Japan	1.3	0.2	0.1	0.1	0.4	1.1	−0.7	−0.8	−0.2	−0.7	−1.2
Germany	0.9	−1.4	−0.2	0.1	−0.3	−0.2	1.1	1.2	1.6	0.1	−0.2
France	0.2	−1.2	0.1	0.8	0.1	0.5	1.4	1.4	2.4	1.7	—
Italy	0.4	−4.1	−1.6	−0.6	0.5	0.4	1.1	1.3	1.9	1.5	0.3
United Kingdom	0.5	−0.9	1.0	1.4	1.1	2.0	1.1	1.3	1.0	0.6	0.4
Canada	1.5	0.8	2.0	1.9	0.8	2.3	2.7	2.8	2.6	1.0	0.8
Other advanced economies	1.4	−0.4	1.3	2.2	1.7	1.5	1.0	2.1	2.1	1.2	0.9
Memorandum											
European Union	0.6	−1.9	−0.2	0.8	0.7	0.9	1.9	1.7	2.0	1.0	0.3
Euro area	0.6	−1.8	−0.5	0.5	0.5	0.8	1.6	1.7	2.0	1.1	0.2
Newly industrialized Asian economies	2.5	1.5	2.8	2.5	2.1	1.6	−2.7	1.5	1.3	1.2	1.4
Unemployment rate											
Advanced economies	**7.0**	**7.5**	**7.4**	**7.1**	**7.1**	**6.9**	**6.8**	**6.4**	**5.8**	**6.0**	**6.6**
Major advanced economies	6.9	7.2	7.0	6.7	6.8	6.6	6.3	6.1	5.7	6.0	6.6
United States[2]	6.8	6.9	6.1	5.6	5.4	5.0	4.5	4.2	4.0	4.9	6.0
Japan	2.5	2.5	2.9	3.2	3.4	3.4	4.1	4.7	4.7	5.0	5.7
Germany	7.3	7.6	8.1	7.9	8.6	9.5	8.9	8.2	7.5	7.5	7.8
France	9.8	11.7	12.3	11.7	12.3	12.3	11.8	11.2	9.5	8.6	8.9
Italy[3]	10.7	10.1	11.1	11.6	11.6	11.7	11.8	11.4	10.6	9.5	9.4
United Kingdom	9.0	10.4	9.7	8.7	8.2	7.1	6.3	6.0	5.6	5.2	5.4
Canada	9.7	11.4	10.4	9.4	9.6	9.1	8.3	7.6	6.8	7.3	8.0
Other advanced economies	7.2	8.6	8.7	8.2	8.1	7.8	8.1	7.3	6.2	6.2	6.3
Memorandum											
European Union	9.4	10.6	11.1	10.7	10.8	10.5	9.8	9.1	8.1	7.6	7.8
Euro area	9.7	10.8	11.5	11.3	11.5	11.5	10.8	10.0	8.9	8.3	8.6
Newly industrialized Asian economies	2.8	2.4	2.2	2.1	2.2	2.5	5.4	5.3	3.8	4.3	4.2

[1]For employment, compound annual rate of change; for unemployment rate, arithmetic average.
[2]The projections for unemployment have been adjusted to reflect the new survey techniques adopted by the U.S. Bureau Labor Statistics in January 1994.
[3]New series starting in 1993, reflecting revisions in the labor force surveys and the definition of unemployment to bring data in line with those of other industrial countries.

Table 3. Inflation
(Percent)

	Average 1983–92	1993	1994	1995	1996	1997	1998	1999	2000	2001	2002
GDP deflator											
Advanced economies	**4.5**	**2.7**	**2.2**	**2.3**	**1.9**	**1.7**	**1.4**	**0.9**	**1.4**	**1.7**	**1.4**
Major advanced economies	3.7	2.3	1.8	1.9	1.6	1.5	1.1	0.9	1.2	1.5	1.3
United States	3.3	2.4	2.1	2.2	1.9	1.9	1.2	1.4	2.3	2.3	2.1
Japan	1.8	0.5	0.1	−0.3	−0.8	0.3	−0.1	−1.4	−1.9	−1.5	−1.5
Germany	2.8	3.7	2.5	2.0	1.0	0.7	1.1	0.5	−0.4	1.4	1.5
France	4.4	2.4	1.8	1.7	1.4	1.2	0.9	0.3	0.8	1.6	1.3
Italy	8.3	3.9	3.5	5.0	5.3	2.4	2.7	1.6	2.2	2.6	1.6
United Kingdom	5.6	2.6	1.4	2.6	3.3	2.9	2.9	2.6	1.7	1.6	2.3
Canada	3.6	1.4	1.2	2.3	1.7	1.1	−0.4	1.4	3.7	1.5	0.7
Other advanced economies	7.9	4.4	3.8	3.9	3.0	2.5	2.3	0.8	1.8	2.3	1.7
Memorandum											
European Union	5.5	3.5	2.7	3.1	2.6	1.9	2.0	1.5	1.5	2.2	1.8
Euro area	5.5	1.9	2.0	2.4	2.9	−0.2	1.2	1.7	1.3	2.3	1.7
Newly industrialized Asian economies	5.4	6.0	5.5	4.7	3.7	2.9	3.2	−2.3	−1.9	0.7	0.9
Consumer prices											
Advanced economies	**4.6**	**3.1**	**2.4**	**2.6**	**2.4**	**2.1**	**1.5**	**1.4**	**2.3**	**2.3**	**1.3**
Major advanced economies	3.9	2.8	2.2	2.2	2.2	2.0	1.3	1.4	2.3	2.2	1.1
United States	4.0	3.0	2.6	2.8	2.9	2.3	1.5	2.2	3.4	2.9	1.6
Japan	1.8	1.3	0.7	−0.1	0.3	1.7	0.7	−0.3	−0.8	−0.7	−1.0
Germany	2.3	4.5	2.7	1.7	1.2	1.5	0.6	0.7	2.1	2.4	1.0
France	4.4	2.1	1.7	1.8	2.1	1.3	0.7	0.6	1.8	1.8	1.1
Italy	7.4	4.6	4.1	5.2	4.0	1.9	2.0	1.7	2.6	2.6	1.3
United Kingdom[1]	5.3	3.0	2.4	2.8	3.0	2.8	2.7	2.3	2.1	2.3	2.4
Canada	4.4	1.8	0.2	1.9	1.6	1.6	1.0	1.7	2.7	2.8	1.6
Other advanced economies	7.7	4.2	3.3	3.8	3.2	2.3	2.4	1.3	2.4	2.9	1.8
Memorandum											
European Union	5.1	3.8	2.6	2.9	2.5	1.8	1.5	1.4	2.3	2.7	1.6
Euro area	5.0	3.9	3.0	2.7	2.3	1.6	1.2	1.1	2.4	2.7	1.4
Newly industrialized Asian economies	4.3	4.6	5.7	4.6	4.3	3.4	4.4	—	1.2	2.0	1.2
Developing countries	**46.4**	**49.2**	**55.4**	**23.2**	**15.4**	**9.9**	**10.5**	**6.8**	**5.9**	**6.0**	**5.3**
Regional groups											
Africa	22.1	39.0	54.7	35.3	30.2	14.2	10.6	11.6	13.5	12.8	8.3
Developing Asia	9.9	10.8	16.0	13.2	8.2	4.8	7.7	2.5	1.9	2.8	3.0
Middle East, Malta, and Turkey	22.9	29.4	37.3	39.1	29.6	27.7	27.6	23.3	19.1	19.1	17.4
Western Hemisphere	170.2	194.6	200.3	36.0	21.2	12.9	9.8	8.8	8.1	6.3	5.2
Analytical groups											
By source of export earnings											
Fuel	15.3	29.2	36.2	42.6	35.1	19.4	17.2	16.2	12.9	13.0	11.8
Nonfuel	51.6	51.8	57.7	21.3	13.5	8.9	9.9	5.9	5.3	5.4	4.8
By external financing source											
Net debtor countries	48.4	51.2	57.5	23.8	15.8	10.2	10.8	6.9	6.1	6.2	5.4
Net debtor countries by debt-servicing experience											
Countries with arrears and/or rescheduling during 1994–98	109.8	200.7	221.8	40.1	21.0	11.9	18.3	13.3	11.0	11.4	8.6
Countries in transition	**42.4**	**635.8**	**274.2**	**133.8**	**42.5**	**27.4**	**21.8**	**43.9**	**20.1**	**16.0**	**11.0**
Central and eastern Europe	...	79.9	45.6	24.7	23.2	41.8	17.1	10.9	12.8	9.3	7.3
CIS and Mongolia	...	1,246.1	508.1	235.6	55.9	19.1	25.0	70.4	25.0	20.6	13.5
Russia	...	878.8	307.5	198.0	47.9	14.7	27.8	85.7	20.8	21.5	14.0
Excluding Russia	...	2,440.9	1,334.5	338.8	75.5	29.7	19.3	41.8	34.6	18.4	12.2
Memorandum											
Median inflation rate											
Advanced economies	4.7	3.0	2.4	2.5	2.2	1.8	1.7	1.5	2.7	2.6	1.9
Developing countries	9.4	9.7	10.6	10.0	7.3	6.2	5.8	4.0	4.2	4.2	4.4
Countries in transition	95.8	472.3	132.1	40.1	24.1	14.8	10.0	8.0	10.0	7.3	5.3

[1]Retail price index excluding mortgage interest.

Table 4. Fiscal Indicators
(Percent of GDP)

	1993	1994	1995	1996	1997	1998	1999	2000	2001	2002
Advanced economies										
Central government balance										
Advanced economies	−4.3	−3.7	−3.3	−2.7	−1.5	−1.7	−0.9	0.3	−0.6	−1.0
United States	−4.2	−3.0	−2.6	−1.8	−0.6	0.5	1.3	2.2	1.0	0.3
Japan	−2.6	−3.4	−3.9	−4.2	−3.9	−8.9	−7.9	−7.5	−6.3	−5.5
Germany	−2.1	−1.5	−1.4	−2.2	−1.7	−1.5	−1.3	1.3	−1.4	−1.1
France	−4.6	−4.6	−4.2	−4.6	−3.6	−3.7	−3.0	−2.4	−1.9	−2.8
Italy	−9.9	−9.1	−7.1	−6.8	−2.9	−2.8	−1.4	−1.0	−2.1	−2.4
United Kingdom	−8.1	−6.9	−5.4	−4.1	−1.5	0.3	1.4	4.0	0.6	−0.1
Canada	−5.4	−4.5	−3.9	−2.0	0.7	1.0	0.9	1.8	0.5	0.5
General government balance										
Advanced economies	−4.7	−4.0	−3.8	−3.1	−1.7	−1.3	−0.9	0.2	−0.9	−1.4
United States	−5.1	−3.8	−3.3	−2.4	−1.3	−0.1	0.6	1.5	0.3	−0.5
Japan	−1.6	−2.2	−3.5	−4.2	−3.2	−4.5	−6.8	−7.9	−7.2	−7.1
Germany[1]	−3.1	−2.4	−3.3	−3.4	−2.7	−2.2	−1.6	1.2	−2.5	−2.5
France[1]	−6.0	−5.5	−5.5	−4.1	−3.0	−2.7	−1.6	−1.4	−0.9	−2.1
Italy[1,2]	−9.4	−9.1	−7.6	−7.1	−2.7	−2.8	−1.8	−0.3	−1.2	−1.0
United Kingdom[1]	−7.7	−6.8	−5.4	−4.1	−1.5	0.3	1.5	3.9	0.5	−0.1
Canada	−8.7	−6.7	−5.3	−2.8	0.2	0.5	1.6	3.2	1.9	1.0
General government structural balance[3]										
Advanced economies	−4.0	−3.4	−3.3	−2.5	−1.3	−0.8	−0.6	−0.5	−0.6	−0.5
United States	−3.8	−2.8	−2.3	−1.5	−0.7	0.1	0.5	1.0	0.5	0.5
Japan	−1.5	−1.9	−3.2	−4.3	−3.4	−3.6	−5.8	−7.0	−5.6	−4.7
Excluding social security	−4.6	−4.7	−6.0	−6.9	−5.9	−6.0	−8.0	−8.7	−7.1	−6.2
Germany[4]	−3.1	−2.5	−3.4	−2.8	−1.7	−1.3	−0.8	−1.3	−1.8	−1.2
France[4]	−3.5	−3.5	−3.7	−1.9	−1.0	−1.5	−0.9	−1.2	−1.2	−1.4
Italy[4]	−8.2	−7.8	−7.0	−6.2	−1.7	−1.8	−0.6	−0.7	−0.5	−0.6
United Kingdom[4]	−6.4	−5.7	−4.6	−3.3	−0.9	0.5	1.5	1.7	0.5	0.1
Canada	−4.3	−3.8	−2.8	—	2.1	2.5	2.5	3.3	2.6	2.7
Developing countries										
Central government balance										
Weighted average	−3.3	−2.8	−2.6	−2.1	−2.4	−3.8	−4.2	−3.0	−3.8	−3.7
Median	−4.2	−3.8	−3.3	−2.4	−2.4	−3.1	−3.4	−2.9	−3.7	−3.4
General government balance										
Weighted average	−3.4	−3.7	−3.3	−3.3	−3.5	−5.0	−5.2	−3.9	−4.8	−4.5
Median	−3.7	−3.4	−3.3	−2.6	−2.4	−3.1	−3.2	−2.9	−3.3	−3.0
Countries in transition										
Central government balance	−6.2	−7.4	−4.6	−4.6	−4.7	−3.5	−2.0	—	−0.2	−1.5
General government balance	−6.8	−7.5	−4.7	−5.9	−5.4	−4.9	−2.2	0.2	−0.8	−2.3

[1]Includes one-off receipts from the sale of mobile telephone licences equivalent to 2.5 percent of GDP in 2000 for Germany, 0.5 percent of GDP in 2001 for France, 1.2 percent of GDP in 2000 for Italy, and 2.4 percent of GDP in 2000 for the United Kingdom.
[2]Includes asset sales equivalent to 0.2 percent of GDP in 2001, 0.7 percent in 2002, 0.5 percent in 2003, and 0.1 percent in 2004.
[3]Percent of potential GDP.
[4]Excludes mobile telephone license receipts.

Table 5. World Trade

(Annual percent change)

	Average 1983–92	1993	1994	1995	1996	1997	1998	1999	2000	2001	2002
Trade in goods and services											
World trade[1]											
Volume	5.4	3.6	8.8	9.8	6.8	10.3	4.2	5.4	12.4	1.0	2.1
Price deflator											
In U.S. dollars	2.2	−3.9	2.7	8.9	−1.3	−5.9	−4.9	−1.6	−0.8	−3.0	0.2
In SDRs	−0.3	−3.1	0.2	2.8	3.1	−0.7	−3.5	−2.3	2.9	0.3	−0.4
Volume of trade											
Exports											
Advanced economies	5.8	2.9	8.6	8.4	6.1	10.5	3.9	5.2	11.6	−0.3	0.5
Developing countries	5.9	9.4	11.3	10.9	9.3	13.3	4.9	4.7	15.0	3.4	4.5
Imports											
Advanced economies	6.5	1.3	9.4	8.7	6.4	9.3	5.9	7.7	11.5	−0.3	1.4
Developing countries	3.3	10.7	6.8	19.6	9.4	10.6	−1.4	1.7	16.1	5.0	6.5
Terms of trade											
Advanced economies	1.1	0.8	0.1	0.2	−0.2	−0.5	1.4	−0.3	−2.3	0.1	0.7
Developing countries	−2.7	−1.7	0.9	3.0	1.8	−1.3	−7.3	3.9	7.5	−2.6	−3.0
Trade in goods											
World trade[1]											
Volume	5.6	4.2	10.0	10.5	6.4	10.5	4.6	5.6	12.8	0.2	1.7
Price deflator											
In U.S. dollars	2.0	−4.6	2.7	9.3	−1.3	−6.2	−5.8	−1.5	0.3	−2.7	0.1
In SDRs	−0.4	−3.7	0.1	3.1	3.2	−1.0	−4.4	−2.3	4.0	0.5	−0.5
Volume of trade											
Exports											
Advanced economies	6.1	3.2	9.6	9.1	5.7	10.8	4.3	5.1	11.8	−0.9	0.4
Developing countries	6.0	9.2	11.8	12.3	9.1	12.6	4.8	4.7	15.4	2.3	3.5
Imports											
Advanced economies	6.8	2.1	11.0	9.3	5.8	9.9	5.9	8.5	11.8	−1.0	1.1
Developing countries	3.4	12.0	7.9	20.1	9.7	10.0	0.5	0.8	16.4	3.5	5.7
World trade prices in U.S. dollars[2]											
Manufactures	4.7	−5.7	3.1	10.3	−3.1	−8.0	−1.9	−1.8	−5.1	−1.7	1.9
Oil	−5.2	−11.8	−5.0	7.9	18.4	−5.4	−32.1	37.5	56.9	−14.0	−23.7
Nonfuel primary commodities	0.8	1.7	13.4	8.4	−1.3	−3.0	−14.7	−7.0	1.8	−5.5	1.7
Terms of trade											
Advanced economies	1.1	1.6	0.5	0.3	−0.8	−0.6	1.6	—	−2.6	−0.2	0.9
Developing countries	−3.2	−3.3	1.4	2.2	2.8	−0.9	−6.6	4.7	7.0	−3.0	−3.3
Fuel exporters	−7.5	−7.0	−1.5	6.1	17.3	0.2	−26.2	30.4	40.5	−10.9	−15.7
Nonfuel exporters	−0.5	−1.6	2.4	2.1	−0.8	−1.1	−1.3	−0.5	−1.3	−0.5	0.4
Memorandum											
World exports in billions of U.S. dollars											
Goods and services	2,877.6	4,725.9	5,286.9	6,266.0	6,587.2	6,852.4	6,768.9	6,970.9	7,746.4	7,556.6	7,689.1
Goods	2,306.8	3,725.1	4,206.1	5,038.3	5,272.0	5,475.9	5,379.1	5,549.5	6,253.3	6,064.0	6,147.9

[1]Average of annual percent change for world exports and imports. The estimates of world trade comprise, in addition to trade of advanced economies and developing countries (which is summarized in the table), trade of countries in transition.

[2]As represented, respectively, by the export unit value index for the manufactures of the advanced economies; the average of U.K. Brent, Dubai, and West Texas Intermediate crude oil spot prices; and the average of world market prices for nonfuel primary commodities weighted by their 1987–89 shares in world commodity exports.

Table 6. Payments Balances on Current Account
(Billions of U.S. dollars)

	1993	1994	1995	1996	1997	1998	1999	2000	2001	2002
Advanced economies	**66.6**	**24.5**	**47.7**	**30.5**	**77.0**	**28.0**	**−139.5**	**−253.7**	**−199.6**	**−197.7**
Major advanced economies	17.0	−14.3	−1.9	−12.8	12.4	−61.8	−221.8	−338.9	−280.6	−272.1
United States	−82.5	−118.2	−109.9	−120.9	−139.8	−217.5	−324.4	−444.7	−392.0	−393.8
Japan	132.0	130.6	111.4	65.8	94.1	121.0	106.8	116.9	90.8	105.7
Germany	−9.8	−23.9	−20.7	−7.9	−2.7	−6.7	−17.9	−19.4	−0.5	13.8
France	9.2	7.4	10.9	20.5	39.4	37.6	37.2	23.8	25.1	20.5
Italy	7.8	13.2	25.1	40.0	32.4	20.0	6.3	−5.7	−1.3	−2.2
United Kingdom	−17.9	−10.4	−14.2	−13.6	−2.8	−8.0	−30.9	−27.9	−24.3	−30.8
Canada	−21.8	−13.0	−4.4	3.4	−8.2	−8.3	1.1	18.1	21.6	14.7
Other advanced economies	49.6	38.8	49.6	43.3	64.6	89.9	82.3	85.2	81.0	74.4
Memorandum										
European Union	8.9	10.1	46.2	77.2	107.8	63.4	6.6	−28.0	0.9	2.7
Euro area[1]	24.7	17.0	53.6	81.3	102.5	64.4	26.1	−8.7	14.2	21.3
Newly industrialized Asian economies	20.8	16.1	5.9	−0.9	10.7	68.0	66.1	50.6	44.1	39.0
Developing countries	**−118.2**	**−85.5**	**−97.1**	**−74.0**	**−58.5**	**−86.7**	**−11.6**	**61.5**	**4.6**	**−69.0**
Regional groups										
Africa	−11.1	−11.5	−16.6	−5.1	−7.0	−20.0	−15.4	3.8	−3.6	−14.2
Developing Asia	−33.0	−19.0	−43.8	−38.8	8.9	47.2	46.2	45.7	24.2	6.2
Middle East, Malta, and Turkey	−28.2	−2.9	−0.2	10.3	6.6	−23.2	14.5	60.8	40.0	−5.8
Western Hemisphere	−46.0	−52.2	−36.5	−40.5	−67.1	−90.7	−56.9	−48.7	−56.0	−55.3
Analytical groups										
By source of export earnings										
Fuel	−23.7	−3.3	2.2	31.4	20.6	−29.7	18.4	97.8	50.9	−0.3
Nonfuel	−94.6	−82.2	−99.2	−105.4	−79.1	−57.0	−30.0	−36.2	−46.3	−68.8
By external financing source										
Net debtor countries	−103.1	−78.1	−99.1	−86.9	−69.7	−71.3	−24.9	4.2	−30.0	−67.9
of which, official financing	−8.0	−9.8	−11.6	−8.7	−4.9	−10.1	−6.5	3.9	−0.9	−10.8
Net debtor countries by debt-servicing experience										
Countries with arrears and/or rescheduling during 1994–98	−28.2	−18.6	−47.3	−41.5	−49.4	−58.4	−23.5	8.5	−17.2	−34.1
Countries in transition	**−7.9**	**2.3**	**−2.2**	**−16.8**	**−23.9**	**−29.1**	**−2.1**	**27.0**	**13.2**	**−6.0**
Central and eastern Europe	−8.1	−3.2	−3.0	−15.0	−16.9	−20.2	−23.1	−19.7	−19.8	−20.7
CIS and Mongolia	0.2	5.5	0.8	−1.9	−7.0	−8.9	21.0	46.7	32.9	14.7
Russia	2.6	8.2	4.9	3.8	−0.4	−1.6	22.7	45.3	33.8	18.0
Excluding Russia	−2.4	−2.7	−4.1	−5.7	−6.6	−7.3	−1.7	1.5	−0.8	−3.3
Total[2]	**−59.5**	**−58.7**	**−51.6**	**−60.3**	**−5.4**	**−87.8**	**−153.2**	**−165.1**	**−181.9**	**−272.8**

[1]Calculated as the sum of the balances of individual euro area countries.
[2]Reflects errors, omissions, and asymmetries in balance of payments statistics on current account, as well as the exclusion of data for international organizations and a limited number of countries.

Table 7. Summary of Balance of Payments, Capital Flows, and External Financing
(Billions of U.S. dollars)

	1993	1994	1995	1996	1997	1998	1999	2000	2001	2002
Developing countries										
Balance of payments[1]										
Balance on current account	−118.2	−85.5	−97.1	−74.0	−58.5	−86.7	−11.6	61.5	4.6	−69.0
Balance on goods and services	−93.9	−56.0	−56.6	−43.7	−35.0	−53.7	24.9	111.5	54.7	−14.9
Income, net	−52.6	−57.7	−73.6	−68.1	−69.1	−74.5	−81.5	−97.5	−98.3	−101.9
Current transfers, net	28.2	28.2	33.1	37.8	45.6	41.5	44.9	47.6	48.2	47.7
Balance on capital and financial account	140.4	114.4	122.7	107.6	116.7	112.8	29.6	−45.6	10.9	78.1
Balance on capital account[2]	5.7	5.5	8.1	9.5	13.4	7.6	8.8	4.7	6.9	8.2
Balance on financial account	134.7	108.9	114.6	98.1	103.3	105.2	20.8	−50.4	4.0	70.0
Direct investment, net	48.0	75.3	85.1	107.6	129.7	130.5	126.1	118.3	134.9	109.5
Portfolio investment, net	103.8	99.2	21.8	72.8	42.2	4.8	19.0	−14.4	−18.9	17.6
Other investment, net	22.3	−15.1	74.3	12.4	−11.9	−35.6	−92.4	−93.6	−46.0	−43.3
Reserve assets	−39.5	−50.4	−66.6	−94.7	−56.7	5.4	−31.8	−60.7	−66.0	−13.8
Errors and omissions, net	−22.1	−28.9	−25.6	−33.6	−58.2	−26.1	−18.0	−15.9	−15.5	−9.1
Capital flows										
Total capital flows, net[3]	174.2	159.3	181.2	192.8	160.0	99.8	52.6	10.3	70.0	83.7
Net official flows	45.0	20.9	33.5	4.1	19.7	32.7	22.1	8.1	47.8	30.8
Net private flows[4]	129.2	138.4	147.7	188.7	140.4	67.0	30.5	2.3	22.2	53.0
Direct investment, net	48.0	75.3	85.1	107.6	129.7	130.5	126.1	118.3	134.9	109.5
Private portfolio investment, net	73.6	93.6	15.2	60.8	36.2	−4.3	11.1	−19.7	−17.0	10.0
Other private flows, net	7.5	−30.4	47.4	20.2	−25.6	−59.3	−106.6	−96.4	−95.7	−66.5
External financing[5]										
Net external financing[6]	187.8	174.4	213.9	239.5	251.0	202.8	165.4	155.2	187.6	185.9
Nondebt-creating flows	93.2	100.5	113.6	150.3	168.6	145.0	142.0	145.9	144.2	134.1
Capital transfers[7]	5.7	5.5	8.1	9.5	13.4	7.6	8.8	4.7	6.9	8.2
Foreign direct investment and equity security liabilities[8]	87.5	95.0	105.6	140.8	155.2	137.4	133.2	141.2	137.3	126.0
Net external borrowing[9]	94.6	73.9	100.2	89.1	82.4	57.8	23.4	9.3	43.4	51.7
Borrowing from official creditors[10]	44.4	21.7	31.9	8.8	11.9	28.5	27.3	9.1	43.5	25.4
Of which,										
Credit and loans from IMF[11]	−0.1	−0.8	12.6	−2.9	0.8	8.5	1.3	−6.7	. . .	. . .
Borrowing from banks[12]	19.3	−28.2	20.3	19.8	25.9	28.1	−3.5	8.0	−2.0	7.7
Borrowing from other private creditors	30.8	80.4	48.0	60.5	44.5	1.2	−0.4	−7.8	1.9	18.6
Memorandum										
Balance on goods and services in percent of GDP[13]	−2.5	−1.4	−1.3	−0.9	−0.7	−1.1	0.5	2.1	1.0	−0.3
Scheduled amortization of external debt	122.7	127.2	154.7	197.0	240.8	245.1	278.2	276.7	260.9	239.4
Gross external financing[14]	310.5	301.6	368.5	436.5	491.8	447.9	443.6	431.9	448.6	425.2
Gross external borrowing[15]	217.3	201.1	254.9	286.1	323.2	302.9	301.6	285.8	304.3	291.1
Exceptional external financing, net	34.1	20.1	20.5	20.3	16.3	20.1	24.0	19.7	25.5	7.6
Of which,										
Arrears on debt service	4.1	−14.1	−2.4	−0.2	−8.3	3.6	12.9	−22.8	. . .	. . .
Debt forgiveness	1.8	1.3	1.9	5.1	14.3	1.6	2.0	3.7	. . .	. . .
Rescheduling of debt service	22.5	25.1	20.3	15.3	10.4	6.1	11.1	41.4	. . .	. . .
Countries in transition										
Balance of payments[1]										
Balance on current account	−7.9	2.3	−2.2	−16.8	−23.9	−29.1	−2.1	27.0	13.2	−6.0
Balance on goods and services	−8.6	1.2	−5.1	−17.8	−19.0	33.8	3.7	32.2	16.2	−1.2
Income, net	−5.5	−3.1	−1.9	−4.8	−10.8	−73.1	−13.8	−13.2	−13.3	−14.8
Current transfers, net	6.2	4.2	4.7	5.8	5.9	10.1	8.0	8.1	10.2	10.0
Balance on capital and finalcial account	10.3	−1.7	5.8	24.1	27.0	37.0	7.3	−19.7	−11.0	5.5
Balance on capital account[2]	2.5	10.2	0.4	1.2	0.3	0.4	0.2	—	0.1	0.1
Balance on financial account	7.8	−11.9	5.4	22.9	26.6	36.6	7.1	−19.7	−11.1	5.4
Direct investment,net	6.0	5.3	13.1	12.4	15.6	21.6	23.4	22.5	26.7	31.5
Portfolio investment, net	8.7	16.1	14.6	13.4	24.4	12.2	1.8	6.2	6.3	6.5
Other investment, net	4.0	−28.0	15.5	−0.9	−3.9	4.4	−11.0	−27.0	−24.4	−20.0
Reserve assets	−10.9	−5.3	−37.8	−2.0	−9.4	−1.6	−7.1	−21.5	−19.7	−12.5
Errors and omissions, net	−2.4	−0.6	−3.6	−7.2	−3.1	−7.8	−5.3	−7.4	−2.1	0.5

Table 7 *(concluded)*

	1993	1994	1995	1996	1997	1998	1999	2000	2001	2002
Capital flows										
Total capital flows, net[3]	18.7	−6.6	43.1	24.9	36.1	38.2	14.2	1.8	8.6	18.0
Net official flows	−1.1	−11.2	−5.8	2.6	32.9	17.2	0.5	−0.4	1.1	3.0
Net private flows[4]	19.8	4.6	49.0	22.3	3.2	21.0	13.8	2.2	7.6	15.0
Direct investment, net	6.0	5.3	13.1	12.4	15.6	21.6	23.4	22.5	26.7	31.5
Private portfolio investment, net	8.7	16.1	14.6	13.4	8.0	4.0	2.8	4.3	3.6	3.5
Other private flows, net	5.1	−16.8	21.3	−3.5	−20.4	−4.6	−12.4	−24.7	−22.7	−20.0
External financing[5]										
Net external financing[6]	19.0	13.4	32.1	35.4	74.8	56.9	42.8	24.8	29.1	42.9
Nondebt-creating flows	9.8	16.3	14.8	14.7	21.4	24.5	24.4	25.8	29.5	34.6
Capital transfers[7]	2.5	10.2	0.4	1.2	0.3	0.4	0.2	—	0.1	0.1
Foreign direct investment and equity security liabilities[8]	7.2	6.1	14.3	13.5	21.1	24.2	24.2	25.9	29.5	34.5
Net external borrowing[9]	9.2	−2.9	17.3	20.7	53.4	32.4	18.4	−1.1	−0.4	8.3
Borrowing from official creditors[10]	2.0	−5.8	−2.5	2.9	32.9	17.2	0.4	−0.4	1.0	3.0
Of which,										
Credit and loans from IMF[11]	3.7	2.4	4.7	3.7	2.5	5.5	−3.6	−4.2	. . .	. . .
Borrowing from banks[12]	5.6	3.8	−0.8	4.6	4.5	5.2	−1.5	—	1.2	2.2
Borrowing from other private creditors	1.7	−0.9	20.6	13.2	16.0	9.9	19.4	−0.6	−2.6	3.1
Memorandum										
Balance on goods and services in percent of GDP[13]	−1.8	0.2	−0.7	−2.0	−2.1	4.2	0.5	4.4	1.9	−0.1
Scheduled amortization of external debt	25.3	22.4	26.7	25.6	19.3	23.1	27.4	29.2	28.2	29.1
Gross external financing[14]	44.3	35.7	58.8	61.0	94.1	80.0	70.2	53.9	57.3	72.0
Gross external borrowing[15]	34.5	19.5	44.0	46.3	72.7	55.5	45.8	28.1	27.7	37.4
Exceptional external financing, net	20.4	17.3	14.9	13.6	−20.8	7.8	7.7	5.2	0.8	0.4
Of which,										
Arrears on debt service	0.5	3.8	−0.5	1.1	−24.8	5.0	1.8	1.6	. . .	. . .
Debt forgiveness	2.1	—	0.9	0.9	—	—	—	—	. . .	. . .
Rescheduling of debt service	1.4	13.3	13.9	9.9	3.3	2.4	4.7	3.7	. . .	. . .

[1]Standard presentation in accordance with the 5th edition of the International Monetary Fund's *Balance of Payments Manual* (1993).

[2]Comprises capital transfers—including debt forgiveness—and acquisition/disposal of nonproduced, nonfinancial assets.

[3]Comprise net direct investment, net portfolio investment, and other long- and short-term net investment flows, including official and private borrowing. In the standard balance of payments presentation above, total net capital flows are equal to the balance on financial account minus the change in reserve assets.

[4]Because of limitations on the data coverage for net official flows, the residually derived data for net private flows may include some official flows.

[5]As defined in the *World Economic Outlook* (see footnote 6). It should be noted that there is no generally accepted standard definition of external financing.

[6]Defined as the sum of—with opposite sign—the goods and services balance, net income and current transfers, direct investment abroad, the change in reserve assets, the net acquisition of other assets (such as recorded private portfolio assets, export credit, and the collateral for debt-reduction operations), and the net errors and omissions. Thus, net external financing, according to the definition adopted in the *World Economic Outlook*, measures the total amount required to finance the current account, direct investment outflows, net reserve transactions (often at the discretion of the monetary authorities), the net acquisition of nonreserve external assets, and the net transactions underlying the errors and omissions (not infrequently reflecting capital flight).

[7]Including other transactions on capital account.

[8]Debt-creating foreign direct investment liabilities are not included.

[9]Net disbursement of long- and short-term credits, including exceptional financing, by both official and private creditors.

[10]Net disbursement by official creditors, based on directly reported flows and flows derived from information on external debt.

[11]Comprise use of International Monetary Fund resources under the General Resources Account, Trust Fund, and Poverty Reduction and Growth Facility (PRGF).

[12]Net disbursement by commercial banks, based on directly reported flows and cross-border claims and liabilities reported in the International Banking section of the International Monetary Fund's *International Financial Statistics*.

[13]This is often referred to as the "resource balance" and, with opposite sign, the "net resource transfer."

[14]Net external financing plus amortization due on external debt.

[15]Net external borrowing plus amortization due on external debt.

Table 8. External Debt and Debt Service

	1993	1994	1995	1996	1997	1998	1999	2000	2001	2002
					Percent of exports of goods and services					
External debt[1]										
Developing countries	**212.8**	**199.6**	**181.3**	**168.0**	**161.0**	**186.1**	**178.0**	**142.3**	**144.3**	**144.4**
Regional groups										
Africa	271.9	281.0	253.1	228.2	216.0	243.6	228.4	177.2	177.8	185.2
Developing Asia	157.3	140.1	127.5	121.7	116.8	126.3	123.4	98.7	99.2	95.2
Middle East, Malta, and Turkey	195.5	192.3	174.6	154.2	155.7	206.3	187.3	144.8	156.0	174.8
Western Hemisphere	288.0	272.3	251.5	236.6	224.2	257.6	253.8	209.7	207.3	201.3
Analytical groups										
By external financing source										
Net debtor countries	239.1	221.2	200.2	186.1	176.3	197.6	191.5	156.1	156.9	153.0
of which, official financing	381.1	396.8	339.9	297.7	260.6	286.4	260.1	194.8	195.3	204.0
Net debtor countries by debt-servicing experience										
Countries with arrears and/or rescheduling during 1994–98	343.6	329.6	305.1	280.7	264.4	311.6	298.4	235.5	239.5	243.5
Countries in transition	**130.6**	**125.1**	**106.6**	**106.6**	**104.2**	**115.5**	**130.7**	**107.6**	**104.1**	**103.6**
Central and eastern Europe	136.4	120.6	100.6	103.7	98.5	91.0	115.0	105.9	100.2	97.3
CIS and Mongolia	125.7	129.2	112.2	109.3	109.7	150.6	149.8	109.4	108.3	111.4
Russia	171.1	166.1	134.2	132.4	130.6	181.3	170.3	122.1	121.4	126.6
Excluding Russia	32.7	35.5	58.0	55.9	63.4	85.0	105.5	80.7	81.2	83.1
Debt-service payments[2]										
Developing countries	**23.0**	**22.5**	**23.1**	**23.9**	**24.2**	**26.3**	**28.0**	**21.9**	**21.5**	**20.4**
Regional groups										
Africa	27.6	27.5	27.6	23.7	21.3	21.8	20.3	17.3	17.1	18.4
Developing Asia	17.9	17.3	16.5	15.3	15.0	17.8	19.0	13.3	13.4	12.0
Middle East, Malta, and Turkey	12.1	14.0	15.0	17.1	14.4	16.5	15.4	12.2	13.6	14.1
Western Hemisphere	39.4	36.9	40.2	46.1	51.6	51.2	59.0	49.7	46.2	42.7
Analytical groups										
By external financing source										
Net debtor countries	26.0	24.5	25.3	25.9	26.6	28.2	30.6	24.3	23.6	21.9
of which, official financing	34.9	36.9	33.1	24.4	20.2	19.3	17.0	13.9	14.5	13.9
Net debtor countries by debt-servicing experience										
Countries with arrears and/or rescheduling during 1994–98	32.1	29.7	33.5	32.2	36.7	44.3	50.2	33.8	33.1	32.8
Countries in transition	**10.1**	**9.8**	**11.5**	**11.2**	**11.1**	**15.8**	**16.7**	**14.5**	**13.9**	**13.4**
Central and eastern Europe	13.9	15.6	15.8	16.1	15.8	15.5	18.4	19.2	17.0	15.4
CIS and Mongolia	6.9	4.7	7.5	6.8	6.5	16.2	14.7	9.7	10.4	10.9
Russia	9.4	5.6	6.7	6.7	5.7	18.7	15.2	8.5	11.0	12.0
Excluding Russia	1.7	2.4	9.3	7.0	8.1	11.0	13.4	12.3	9.1	9.0
					Billions of U.S. dollars					
Memorandum										
External debt										
Developing countries	1,605.3	1,729.9	1,876.1	1,950.3	2,031.6	2,180.4	2,243.5	2,204.0	2,194.8	2,210.9
Countries in transition	236.3	253.0	275.9	299.1	308.6	360.4	358.4	358.9	364.6	372.9
Debt-service payments										
Developing countries	173.6	194.8	239.5	277.8	305.5	308.0	352.7	339.0	327.6	313.6
Countries in transition	18.2	19.8	29.7	31.4	32.8	49.4	45.8	48.3	48.6	48.2

[1] Total debt at year-end in percent of exports of goods and services in year indicated.

[2] Debt-service payments refer to actual payments of interest on total debt plus actual amortization payments on long-term debt. The projections incorporate the impact of exceptional financing items.

WORLD ECONOMIC OUTLOOK AND STAFF STUDIES FOR THE WORLD ECONOMIC OUTLOOK, SELECTED TOPICS, 1992–2001

I. Methodology—Aggregation, Modeling, and Forecasting

II. Historical Surveys

IV. Inflation and Deflation; Commodity Markets

V. Fiscal Policy

VI. Monetary Policy; Financial Markets; Flow of Funds

VII. Labor Market Issues

VIII. Exchange Rate Issues

IX. External Payments, Trade, Capital Movements, and Foreign Debt

X. Regional Issues

XI. Country-Specific Analyses

Staff Studies for the
World Economic Outlook

World Economic and Financial Surveys

This series (ISSN 0258-7440) contains biannual, annual, and periodic studies covering monetary and financial issues of importance to the global economy. The core elements of the series are the *World Economic Outlook* report, usually published in May and October, and the annual report on *International Capital Markets*. Other studies assess international trade policy, private market and official financing for developing countries, exchange and payments systems, export credit policies, and issues discussed in the *World Economic Outlook*. Please consult the IMF *Publications Catalog* for a complete listing of currently available World Economic and Financial Surveys.

World Economic Outlook: A Survey by the Staff of the International Monetary Fund

The *World Economic Outlook,* published twice a year in English, French, Spanish, and Arabic, presents IMF staff economists' analyses of global economic developments during the near and medium term. Chapters give an overview of the world economy; consider issues affecting industrial countries, developing countries, and economies in transition to the market; and address topics of pressing current interest.

ISSN 0256-6877.

$42.00 (academic rate: $35.00); paper.

2001. (Oct.). ISBN 1-58906-073-3. **Stock #WEO EA 0022001.**
2001. (May). ISBN 1-58906-032-6. **Stock #WEO EA 0012001.**
2000. (Oct.). ISBN 1-55775-975-8. **Stock #WEO EA 0022000.**
2000. (May). ISBN 1-55775-936-7. **Stock #WEO EA 012000.**
1999. (Oct.). ISBN 1-55775-839-5. **Stock #WEO EA 299.**
1999. (May). ISBN 1-55775-809-3. **Stock #WEO-199.**

Official Financing for Developing Countries
by a staff team in the IMF's Policy Development and Review Department led by Anthony R. Boote and Doris C. Ross

This study provides information on official financing for developing countries, with the focus on low-income countries. It updates the 1995 edition and reviews developments in direct financing by official and multilateral sources.

$25.00 (academic rate: $20.00); paper.

2001. ISBN 1-58906-038-5. **Stock #WEO EA 0132001.**
1998. ISBN 1-55775-702-X. **Stock #WEO-1397.**
1995. ISBN 1-55775-527-2. **Stock #WEO-1395.**

Exchange Rate Arrangements and Currency Convertibility: Developments and Issues
by a staff team led by R. Barry Johnston

A principle force driving the growth in international trade and investment has been the liberalization of financial transactions, including the liberalization of trade and exchange controls. This study reviews the developments and issues in the exchange arrangements and currency convertibility of IMF members.

$20.00 (academic rate: $12.00); paper.

1999. ISBN 1-55775-795-X. **Stock #WEO EA 0191999.**

World Economic Outlook Supporting Studies
by the IMF's Research Department

These studies, supporting analyses and scenarios of the *World Economic Outlook*, provide a detailed examination of theory and evidence on major issues currently affecting the global economy.

$25.00 (academic rate: $20.00); paper.

2000. ISBN 1-55775-893-X. **Stock #WEO EA 0032000.**

International Capital Markets: Developments, Prospects, and Key Policy Issues
by a staff team led by Donald J. Mathieson and Garry J. Schinasi

This year's *International Capital Markets* report assesses recent developments in mature and emerging financial markets and analyzes key systemic issues affecting global financial markets. The report discusses the main risks in the period ahead; identifies sources of, and possible measures to avoid, instability in OTC derivatives markets; reviews initiatives to "involve"the private sector in preventing and resolving crises, and discusses the role of foreign-owned banks in emerging markets.

$42.00 (academic rate: $35.00); paper

2001. ISBN 1-58906-056-3. **Stock #WEO EA 0062001.**
2000. (Sep.). ISBN 1-55775-949-9. **Stock #WEO EA 0062000**
1999. (Sep.). ISBN 1-55775-852-2. **Stock #WEO EA 699.**
1998. (Sep.). ISBN 1-55775-770-4. **Stock #WEO-698**

Toward a Framework for Financial Stability
by a staff team led by David Folkerts-Landau and Carl-Johan Lindgren

This study outlines the broad principles and characteristics of stable and sound financial systems, to facilitate IMF surveillance over banking sector issues of macroeconomic significance and to contribute to the general international effort to reduce the likelihood and diminish the intensity of future financial sector crises.

$25.00 (academic rate: $20.00); paper.

1998. ISBN 1-55775-706-2. **Stock #WEO-016.**

Trade Liberalization in IMF-Supported Programs
by a staff team led by Robert Sharer

This study assesses trade liberalization in programs supported by the IMF by reviewing multiyear arrangements in the 1990s and six detailed case studies. It also discusses the main economic factors affecting trade policy targets.

$25.00 (academic rate: $20.00); paper.

1998. ISBN 1-55775-707-0. **Stock #WEO-1897.**

Private Market Financing for Developing Countries
by a staff team from the IMF's Policy Development and Review Department led by Steven Dunaway

This study surveys recent trends in flows to developing countries through banking and securities markets. It also analyzes the institutional and regulatory framework for developing country finance; institutional investor behavior and pricing of developing country stocks; and progress in commercial bank debt restructuring in low-income countries.

$20.00 (academic rate: $12.00); paper.

1995. ISBN 1-55775-526-4. **Stock #WEO-1595.**

Available by series subscription or single title (including back issues); academic rate available only to full-time university faculty and students. For earlier editions please inquire about prices.

The IMF *Catalog of Publications* is available on-line at the Internet address listed below.

Please send orders and inquiries to:
International Monetary Fund, Publication Services, 700 19th Street, N.W.
Washington, D.C. 20431, U.S.A.
Tel.: (202) 623-7430   Telefax: (202) 623-7201
E-mail: publications@imf.org
Internet: http://www.imf.org